THE POWER OF THE PASSPORT

MY YEAR AWAY FROM AMERICA

THE POWER OF THE PASSPORT

MY YEAR AWAY FROM AMERICA

Mark A. Cooper II

The Power Of The Passport / Mark A. Cooper II - 1st ed.

ISBN: 978-0-9965817-9-0

1. International Travel 2. Basketball 3. Adventure 4. Culture
First Edition
Printed in United States of America

DEDICATION

To My Grandfather, George Jenkins Sr.
and
Uncle George Jenkins Jr.

Table of Contents

ACKNOWLEDGMENTS

First, I want to thank God for enabling me to go on my international journey and guiding me through difficult decisions while traveling through many countries. Of course, many thanks to my family for their support and help during my international travels. To the editors of this book, I am sincerely appreciative for helping me bring this project to life. I would like to acknowledge the great people that I met during my journey outside the States. Without your kindness and hospitality, the concept of this book would not have even been imagined. To everyone who has pushed me to grow as a person, with either positive or negative energy, thank you.

INTRODUCTION

As I neared the end of my stay in Europe, I was struck with the idea to write a book about my travels. I was so amazed at the people and places I had encountered, and how vivid their stories were, that I felt compelled to tell others. In my earlier years, I would have been comfortable simply keeping those memories to myself, quietly enjoying the fact that there was an incredibly vast world that I could visit when I wanted to. However, this mindset changed when I watched an old Tupac Shakur interview. In it, he said, "I have to repay for that blessing…by shining. If He [God] gives you the voltage, and you waste it…that's the curse." It became clear to me that God did not send me on this eye-opening journey to keep the memories to myself, but instead, He had given me an assignment to bring these stories back home and share what I had learned. As I realized this, I also came to recognize the personal growth that had taken place in me. I was no longer the reserved athlete that I once had been.

The initial concept was to keep it simple and name this book My Year Away from America, but as my ideas developed, I was able to see that this book was much bigger than me, and it should focus on the things and the people that helped me get to these places. Travel has always been viewed as a wonderful privilege, but there isn't much of an emphasis on how much power a passport has. A passport is the initial key to international treasures such as the world's wonders and different cultures, but outside of rich communities, possessing one is rarer. It's more of a "great if you have one" situation, but not looked on as a necessity. I'm honestly not sure how long it would have taken me to get a passport if my mother had not forced me to get mine for a trip to visit my sister in London.

The first time I traveled across the Atlantic Ocean was with my mom and my friend to visit my sister in London, England. If I'm being completely honest, at first, I was not thrilled to go. This was in 2007, before Instagram and all the popular social networks gave you a greater chance to see other people experiencing new places. I seriously thought London would be like the pictures of Stonehenge I'd seen—just green grass surrounding ancient ruins, and nothing more. Whenever I saw royal parties or ceremonies, I never saw any people of color, which led me to believe I would dislike London because I would not fit in. Of course, when we arrived in London, I learned otherwise. I was shocked to find that the environment was not that different from New York. I couldn't believe that my expectations were so far from the truth. This single experience changed my views about what the rest of the world looks and feels like.

I made a strong effort to be as transparent as possible while writing this book, because I wanted to show that a lot of my trips weren't planned, and many of the problems I faced were unforeseen. I believe that my many impromptu decisions made the trip better. I was able to let God guide the way, which took the pressure off of me when it came to worrying about the future. If I had scheduled and booked all the necessary flights and hotels for my trip, I may have become jaded, bored, or tired of a certain place. The lack of a strict schedule gave me the versatility to change the pace or direction whenever I felt led to. The end result was a natural journey, and my experiences had more substance because of it.

The main goal of this project is to reach people all over the world, with the hope that the stories will resonate with them and motivate them to obtain passports or use the ones they already have to explore the world. In school, when I learned about the great places of the world in history or social studies class, it never occurred to my adolescent mind that one day I would travel to a site like the Great Pyramids of Giza. The idea of traveling to Africa did not even truly become a strong desire in me until I saw Malcolm X's picture in Egypt. I had only heard Brother Malcolm mention Tanzania, so it sparked a curiosity in me that eventually became a reality. In several of his interviews, he spoke in depth about the plans for unity that he envisioned for Tanzania, but I had only heard him speak briefly of the country in one of his famous speeches. I honestly believe that the more we travel and talk about lesser known countries like Tanzania, the more others we speak to will develop a thirst to travel to them as well. Everyone's financial situation is different, but I believe that motivation and determination are powerful enough to erase that constraint. For myself, I really believed that God was going to open the doors for me to travel and realize what I had dreamed about—as long as I put the work in. The result was God opening doors that I couldn't have even imagined beforehand.

There are many adults today who still do not have a passport, for whatever reason, and it's possible that they are not completely grasping what they are missing out on. As I wrote more chapters, the book developed into a useful tool that would help bring clarity to its readers, rather than just a story book. The stories in this book blow up the stereotypical ideas people may hold about many countries and their cultures. It shows the first-hand encounters that I had with several great people. Due to misinformation, many people in the United States believe that specific countries are extremely unsafe, so I made a serious effort in each of my stories to include details that firmly discredit these harmful myths. It's all too easy to draw conclusions after listening to someone's opinion on television or from reading a newspaper article, but actually traveling to an area for yourself may produce a better experience. In all of the countries I traveled to, almost all of the people were welcoming and exceedingly helpful. I wanted to give a thorough account in these stories to ensure that their kindness and generosity were exemplified.

When I was younger, my first travels outside of the country were to well-known cities that are common travel destinations for most Americans, like London, Rome, and Paris. Those trips that occurred earlier in my twenties led me to wonder if there are less prestigious countries that may be just as pleasant. When I realized how many amazing places there are in Europe and Africa, I had the idea to create BraveVoyage.com, where I could give an account of the countries that I had visited and add to the list as I went along. After living abroad and skipping from country to country, I noticed that I did not see a lot of Americans, specifically Black Americans like myself. In Paris, I could hear about ten different languages, especially around the tourist sections, but very seldom did I hear an American accent. Based on my observations alone, I concluded that many Americans aren't actually traveling to certain countries in Africa and Europe. In various countries on the two continents, I would maybe see one American group in a day, but never more than that. However, it is possible that American tourists were on tour buses, only venturing out when they arrived at the landmarks or their hotels. In my opinion, that type of sightseeing is just as effective online as it is in person.

It's great to see landmarks and works of art that you envisioned when you were younger, but for me, the true bonus is in getting to meet the people of the country and embracing their culture. Anyone can take a picture of the Eiffel Tower and post it online, but being able to share a story about the conversations you had with French people during your walk through Paris is worth even more. A "tourist complex" is the mindset of traveling to a country and believing that everyone at that destination is there to serve you because you paid for a flight and a hotel. This complex is very common among Americans because we're subject to first-class marketing and customer service that isn't common worldwide. If you travel to a country and have a tourist complex, that vibe is easily sensed by the locals, and they may respond negatively. However, if you go with the open mind of meeting new people and learning, then your trip experience might be elevated. Travel tour companies do a great job of marketing safety and keeping a tight itinerary for you, but because of their strict scheduling, you may be missing out on experiences you aren't even aware of. Traveling with a tourism company may also limit your choices, and that may be a reason that many beautiful countries remain hidden treasures.

A 2016 report from the Office of National Travel and Tourism revealed that a total of 66,960,943 US citizens traveled outside of the country in 2015. Of that number, about 37.5 million went to either Mexico or Canada. Europe was next on the list, with about 12 million, then the Caribbean, with 6.5 million, followed by Asia, with 4.3 million. Between 2015 and 2016, international tourism in general was robust, but travel to Africa somehow declined. Although international travel in 2015 was great for other continents, according to the African Development Bank Group, Africa's tourist arrivals dropped from 64.8 million people in 2014 to 62.5 million in 2015. The lack of travel to Africa shocks me, because I think of the great places that I've been to on the continent and the other countries that I still have yet to see. It makes sense that people want to travel to places that might be closer and cheaper, but I'm not completely sure that these are the only reasons for the lopsided statistics. I'm sure that if certain countries had more marketing behind them and had more information shared about them in America, then the numbers would change drastically. The effort to push conversations about less-traveled areas must be increased.

There's a whole world out there, and the more we use the power of the passport for our own advances, the more we can help improve other people individually and our society as a whole. Money and possessions may leave you or lose value over time, but the experiences and connections that you make with people from different backgrounds can have an effect that lasts forever. Traveling may provide you with the opportunity to learn more about yourself and your value in this world. It may also encourage you to let go of labels and stereotypes in order to appreciate others simply for who they are. The goal of this book is to motivate its readers to travel more, by telling how I was able to grow and learn from real encounters that I had while away from my American comfort zone.

CHAPTER 1

THE ROUTE CHANGE

I still remember the empty feeling I had when I was ready to buy my next house. The first two times I had bought properties, I was 100% focused on fixing them up and making them into people's dream homes. I figured that the process on my next house would be a breeze because of the experience that I had gained over the years. Even so, for some reason, there was a nerve in my body that would not allow me to use a significant amount of my money to buy another possession. Everything was lined up perfectly for me to make the purchase, as my cousin, Sherman, was now a realtor and made the process painless. I no longer had a job, so I had the freedom of time to get any project done in a quick fashion. I seemed to be in a perfect position to thrive in America as a young entrepreneur, but there was a feeling in my body that just would not let me move forward.

It took me some time to understand why I felt this way and what it could mean for my future. Was I tired from the last project? Was I unsure that I could do the project without the safety net of income from a steady job? Or was I just feeling guilty because of having financial freedom at what some would deem too early an age? I asked myself all these questions, but they did not seem to match my feelings, or even my personality, for that matter. I do not focus much on the past, and my confidence in my ability to finish projects was stronger than ever after my initial struggles. The guilt about financial freedom seemed possible, but my resources weren't so numerous that I could make a huge financial impact on my community to counteract my guilt.

I spent many nights reflecting on the things I really wanted to do and where I saw myself in five years. Of course, I prayed about it and asked God for direction, but I'm sure that's where the uneasy feeling about buying the house came from, anyway. I read various articles about trying something different and re-inventing one's self to experience new things. I also watched countless motivational YouTube videos that told me to follow my dreams and try something different, rather than chasing money year after year. I was forced to step back and figure out what brought me happiness and what I enjoyed doing most.

I slowly began to realize that most of the things that we do for pleasure, we usually do to get away from our jobs and our problems. Whether it's a major vacation across the sea or a small trip across state lines, we are usually doing it to escape from our jobs. When I was renovating my first house, I had a full time job at the bank. Sometimes, I would even leave during my lunch break, just to get a little bit of work done. Then, after my day job, I would come home immediately and spend all night working on my house. By the time I started working on my second house, I realized that the renovations were a form of therapy for my day job. It seemed like many customers and co-workers would bring their problems to me, and I had to share in their misery. I developed a love for the peacefulness of working by myself in my house, and it became addictive. However, once I was able to leave my job, that balance was no longer present, and it was time to search for a higher level of satisfaction.

My hunger for more out of life is easy to explain, due to the hardships that I endured while trying to maintain a nine-to-five career. This process first started when I graduated college. At that time, jobs in the marketing field were scarce, because of the financial crisis of 2008. That long stretch of being unemployed—when just a few months before I had graduated and felt like I was on top of the world—wore me down every day, starting when I woke up. I woke up day after day wondering, "Is this the day somebody calls me and realizes I'm special?" I was deeply longing to be a part of a workforce that I really knew nothing about, except that it paid money, and that's what I had always been told makes you feel better.

After working small jobs and renovating houses with my uncle, I landed a bank teller job, which launched me into another stage of disappointment called "underemployment." So, after days of waking up without any perceived purpose, I had now found a job where I was heading to work every day and not being challenged. I'm honestly not sure which state of mind is worse, because the underemployment can consistently serve you disappointment and train you to expect less, while unemployment makes you wonder if anybody thinks you are valuable. I began to think that if I were able to get a better job with a great company, then my disappointments would wash away, and I could finally start living the "American

Dream." I prayed often for a great job with a wonderful organization, where everybody would be amiable. The last financial institution that I worked for was the closest I ever got to that, but it was far from perfect. It became clear that I was never going to be content with my situation until I was working on my own terms and working on my own time.

The transition from a job to working for myself was not easy and required many long days and nights. Once God gave me the vision for a path out of my job, I worked tirelessly to reach that destination. My trials and tribulations with real estate are a dozen chapters made for a completely different book, but in short, it was not a straightforward process. Like a nine-to-five job, there were setbacks and extremely tough days, and they were always my fault. Even so, no matter what went wrong, it gave me pride that the project was mine and the success of the project depended on my will. The hard work and dedication eventually paid off, and the journey to freedom from a day job was finally complete.

Since I now had freedom from work, I was able to coach basketball a lot more in my hometown of Philadelphia. Coaching kids in basketball is a form of therapy for me, and it will never get old, because I always see myself in the kids I coach. Through coaching, I was able to witness the happiness in human beings at an early age, and how the smallest things bring them sincere joy. These observations were especially significant to me after five years of working with unhappy coworkers who seemed to be burnt out and did not have many reasons to smile during our eight hours together. It may not be the case during the actual gameplay, but basketball has always brought a calm to my life and it allows me to forget all of the things that I may see as hardship. Being able to watch the kids find the highest level of joy and laughter took me back to a time when life was pure joy.

Even though I was not getting paid to do it, coaching the kids was a form of work, and I embraced my duty of responsibility. Working with kids showed me the difference in the work ethic between a child and an adult when trying to achieve a goal. When children make up their mind to get better at something, they'll do whatever it takes to improve themselves, especially if someone is there to guide them. When I worked with adults, I noticed that even though they wanted to advance in their careers, they would often look for ways to get further ahead with less work. Children usually have a set goal, and they will do anything to reach it. The more adults I worked with, the more I realized that a majority of them just want to be able to pay their bills, and they'll most likely take any job if it appears to be better than their last.

It was always a dream of mine to travel the world and play basketball, so why not do both simultaneously? I'd always thought about taking the journey, but a lack of knowledge on the steps to complete an objective will always scare people away from following through on a desire. I've read several reviews on journeys to play basketball overseas, and I'd had my own experiences on joining "combine programs," but I figured I would do it my own way. The combine programs consisted of a participant paying money to someone who supposedly had connections with foreign agents, teams, and coaches, and then showcasing their talent for them with the hopes of earning a contract. This was the best time to embark on a serious journey to the destinations of my choice. I was 27, with no kids, and had sufficient funds to cover any expenses. I had to ask myself, "Even if this does not feel like the best time, when could it possibly be a better time?" After making up my mind, I instantly had the zeal to plan out my travels throughout Europe and Africa. I imagined all the places I had dreamed about going to since I was a kid and strategized on how could I squeeze them all into one trip. I compiled a list of countries that I had always wanted to visit and others that I was just curious about. There are distinct nations that you hear about in the news or see pictures in wanderlust articles, but I honestly wondered what it would be like to see them in person.

I had already done a good share of traveling at this point and had seen many places that were close to the USA. But I wanted this trip to be beyond most imaginations, to the point where it would seem out of the norm to some people. In the previous year, I had tested myself to see if I really could be away from America for a long time, when I stayed in Paris for a month. My desire to stay in Paris stemmed from a group trip I had taken there with two childhood friends that lasted about a week and a half. Paris had a tremendous impact on my life, and I was amazed at how easily I took to the city and the people. The second trip to Paris, by myself, gave me confidence that I could live away from America for more than a month, so it was time to see how much further I could go.

The more I planned the trip, the more I concluded that I was making the right decision. A bright light formed in my mind, filling me with the desire to experience new places and possibly grow as a person. Of course, the whole trip would end up strengthening my faith in God, because I did not know anybody in these countries and had never been to most of them. Even so, I had learned in the past that the farther I went with faith, the more doors would open for me.

Looking at the top destinations on my list, my first priority was safety. Since I was a kid, I've always fantasized about going to Egypt and seeing the Great Pyramids of Giza. However, in recent years, I kept hearing news about the unrest in Cairo and the riots in the center of the city. When I had a job, I would constantly check the travel safety alert on Cairo to see if the alert level had been lowered, but that never happened. I had also planned to take one of the faith-based tours offered by a tour company, but during this time, most companies had stopped booking tours to Egypt because of the riots. There was a client at my job who was actually from Egypt, and she would warn me about going there because it was far too dangerous. I took this as a serious warning, but then I remembered that my hometown of Philadelphia isn't necessarily the safest place in the world. It may not seem true to most people, but I calculated that any chance of danger in Egypt could be the same as in Philadelphia.

Another destination on my list was Israel, specifically Tel Aviv and Jerusalem. Israel is a country with many inbound travelers, but it's usually in difficult times with the countries that border it. I followed the same method that I had with Egypt, by checking the travel safety alerts, and the rhetoric was more of the same.

Ironically, a documentary on Israel's dangerous present times was shown at my church some weeks before I left. It was an in-depth documentary talking about the plot of all the powers in the world to try and destroy Israel. All I could think was, "Great, this is the place I'm planning to travel to, simply for the tourism."

Nonetheless, visiting Israel had always been a huge desire for me, as I was raised in the church and was well aware of all the biblical stories and cities of Israel. Based on my background alone, Israel was a no-brainer, and for some reason, I was not deterred at all after seeing the disturbing documentary. Having learned and been immersed in the biblical stories since I was a toddler, it only made sense to actually see these places for myself.

Other than those two places, I had never had any other strong desires to go anywhere outside of Europe or the Caribbean. I usually learned about places from studying historical figures that I consider to be my heroes. I once read about Malcolm X's travels to Zanzibar, Tanzania, and his other journeys to places in Africa. I'm sure it was difficult to picture back in the 1960s, but with Google Images at my fingertips, I was able to see how great these places were. My curiosity quickly turned into research, and from there, into a geography lesson. I began to educate myself on the world map as I strategized which connecting countries would be the most cost efficient to travel between. I saw that Kenya and Tanzania were next to each other, so it would make sense to try a safari tour and then see Mt. Kilimanjaro. When I say "see," I mean drive to the mountain and maybe climb up a few hundred yards. I'm highly adventurous, but not to the extreme where I'm putting my life in jeopardy. This strategy also gave me the option of going to Ethiopia as well, because the countries are right beside each other. I did not know much about the current Ethiopian culture, but after some brief research, the landmarks and history in Ethiopia intrigued me.

The only other countries that I had ever strongly desired to visit were South Africa, Morocco, and the Congo. I considered South Africa because of its versatility—it has everything from history to beaches to safaris. My interest in Morocco was because I had always heard of the great city of Marrakech, and I figured a chance to be surrounded by the culture would be too amazing an opportunity to pass up. After reading up on Patrice Lumumba some years back, I had developed a deep interest in learning about the Congo and its current events. The only issue that would deter me from going to the Congo was that many people told me that it was not safe at all because of armed groups and paramilitary operations. Thus, my plans to visit the Congo seemed too far-fetched at the time, but I still kept a hope that it would one day be possible.

Now that my list of core countries was complete, I figured I could squeeze in other destinations through a combination of layovers and taking advantage of extra time and flight deals. When factoring in the possibility of something going wrong, it seemed like too much of a gamble to take a trip that was completely structured and already mapped out. Anything could go wrong, and I did not want to be obligated to go to a certain place, because situations can change quickly. In addition, prices fluctuate, so my method would give me the option to choose where I could navigate my trips, based on what day I was ready to leave. It also gave me the ability to buy time on my decision when it came to what countries I wanted to travel to.

I'm usually a private person when it comes to dreams, goals, and journeys, so I tried to keep my plans to myself and my family as much as possible. I almost thought about just simply leaving and calling people when I reached my first destination, but my family probably would've disapproved and possibly told me not to come back. Instead, I ran the idea by my family and some of my friends, and everyone seemed to be supportive. The most common response was, "There's never going to be a better time," a comment that often came from the older folks that I know. Of course, there was some discomfort about traveling to some of these countries, due to their unknown safety conditions. When you plan to travel anywhere in Africa or Europe, the number one question you might hear is, "Is it safe there?" In an effort to show transparency, I cannot act like safety does not bother me at times, but in my travels, I have rarely encountered people with evil intentions. Of course, you have your pick-pockets and sneaky thieves everywhere, but I have never felt in true danger. In comparison, there are tons of neighborhoods in my city alone that I would deem unsafe to walk in. That guides my logic for a lot of my choices when I ask myself if it is safe.

Somehow, I almost forgot that I had to get travel vaccines and obtain paperwork in order to voyage through Africa. I did as much research as I could to see if they were even necessary, or if I could somehow chance it and avoid the shots. To make a long story short: No, I couldn't. It was not possible at all to avoid these vaccines, and I would also need to go through a little class on the different health problems I might be faced with. I heard about one company that administers the vaccines, and I visited the office to learn more about what vaccines would be mandatory. The office was professional, and the information provided was helpful, but I still ended up meeting with my first roadblock—the price. After listing all the countries that I had planned to travel to, the total cost for the vaccinations came to around $1500. The price I had in mind would only set me back about $150. Truthfully, this is one point where I seriously considered putting off the trip until another time. I had failed to factor in the high cost of vaccines, and at the time, it did not seem to make sense to spend the price of maybe three flights "just" for vaccines.

I had a legitimate excuse as to why I couldn't travel, and I was reaching the point of giving up, but I convinced myself to at least search for other options. I found that that agency was not the only facility where I could go for vaccinations, and that I did not necessarily have to get every shot. Through more research, I realized that the administration of vaccines is also a business, and a lot of the information I was given was, in part, to scare me and "sell me up," so I would pay for more vaccines than needed. It's very easy to sell someone mosquito repellent and accessories when the Zika virus is all over the news. Whenever planning a trip to Africa, I urge anybody to research the countries that you are going to and verify the required vaccines and paperwork that you'll need.

I found an agency that had lower prices for their vaccines, so I asked for the doctor's opinion on the ones that I would definitely need for the specific countries I planned to travel to. Based on my research and the doctor's suggestions, the cost was significantly lower than the first estimate that I was quoted. I decided that I would go through with the vaccines, and my trip was back on schedule. After getting my shots, I received my yellow international certificate of vaccination from the World Health Organization and prepared to start the structuring of my quest.

Everything was in line for my trip, and the last step was to actually book the flights and hotels. I'd convinced myself to navigate the travel route without much planning ahead, but I was not sure what would be the first stop on the itinerary. I searched flights to all of the destinations from all of the airports within the Philadelphia, New York City, and DC area. The price that seemed the most logical was a flight from John F. Kennedy Airport in New York to Tel Aviv, Israel. After watching a documentary on how dangerous Israel could potentially be, it was probably best to get that out of the way first before anything else happened. Ironically, I had to seriously pray about going to the Holy Land. It would look rather idiotic to get in a bad situation in a foreign country when I had previously been given a warning at church about the country's current state. When the flight came available for me, I perceived it as a sign that I should go.

The only other flight I wanted to book was for the second destination, because I did not want to be too unorganized. I figured Egypt would be a fairly cheap flight from Israel. However, I found out that the best option between Tel Aviv and Cairo was a stop in Athens, Greece. I really had no intention of stopping in Europe for very long, but I realized that this was a great chance to add a stopover to the trip and see another historic city. Luckily, the timing was optimal to go to Greece in terms of getting the most "bang for my buck." Greece had recently gone through some changes with their economy, and it was rather cheap at that moment for tourists to have a great time.

I usually never stress about staying in a high-end hotel, and I never have had the need to be in a certain area, because I do not plan to stay in the room when I'm traveling. Reviews on hotels are easy to find online, so as long as it looks clean and the reviews match, I'm sold. Unless you are a "high roller," I suggest that you find hotels with good beds and nice bathrooms and forego the costly extras. All else is just for vanity and only to show off on social networks. If you have the opportunity to travel to the great wonders of the world and explore amazing cities, there's really no need to spend extra money on a hotel that you'll only sleep in. One reason I say that is because of the money, but another reason is that staying in a plush hotel may kill your motivation to get out and see the city. I decided to go to Cairo to see the Pyramids, not for a hotel's bed sheet count.

After shopping for the various things I needed for travel and visiting relatives, I was ready to go. I tried to be as clear as I could and tell them that I would be traveling for a while. Word about my future expedition went around fast, and the Sunday before I left, my church announced my plans and prayed for me during service.

As I said before, I'm a rather private person, but I was very thankful for the prayers and well wishes of my friends and family in my community. I'm usually reluctant to talk about my travels, because sometimes I find it embarrassing to be so blessed to be able to see the world. It's great to be able to give a testimony of how much God has blessed you, but in today's age of social media, there's usually a thin line between a testimony and bragging. But for the most part, everybody was happy for me, and I knew that this trip had to be more than just an experience for myself. I was going for the people who may have never had the idea, or who did not know what the first step was to going. I was also traveling for the people who, unfortunately, will never be able to travel to see these great places. Those are some simple understandings that I carry with myself when I travel throughout the world.

I said my final goodbyes and headed to New York City for my overnight flight to Tel Aviv, Israel. I had never heard of Azerbaijan Airlines before, but I'm never really picky when taking flights. I had figured that all of the difficult parts of preparing for my trip were completed, but I was sadly mistaken. When I arrived at John F. Kennedy Airport for my 11 PM flight, I did not see the airline staff. I searched the entire terminal, and Azerbaijan's staff was nowhere in sight, there was not even any signage. I assumed that I had possibly stopped at the wrong terminal, but the terminal list said I was at the correct stop. I went to ask an agent from another airline, and they told me that their flights usually leave by a certain time during the day. I checked my emails, and sure enough, I had read the international times wrong. It's a rather small airline, so something as simple as an online check-in or an alert email was not available. My advice to anyone using the service of a smaller airline is to make sure you check everything yourself and call or email in advance to confirm everything.

I was in a dilemma, because there were no more flights to my destination for the night, and I was in New York City, not Philadelphia. I have family and friends in New York, but it was about 10:00 at night, and no one was answering their phone. Once again, I was faced with another tough decision to make. Maybe the trip just was not meant to be, and I could just save a bunch of money by going back home on a late Megabus and plan it for later. No great sum of money would be lost, because I only booked the first flight to allow myself flexibility of schedule. I prayed about it and decided that if I saw a reasonable flight leaving the next day, then I would consider going through with the trip. Fortunately, I found an early flight and I was able to book it for the next day.

The next small problem was my sleeping arrangements for the night. I could find a hotel, but it did not make sense to only stay there for five hours and have to worry about waking up to get back to the airport in time. I made the decision to stay in the airport terminal and found a comfortable seat. Thank God it was not a "crazy night" at my terminal, and I did not have to act accordingly. It was not a night that held much rest for me, but I survived. The next day, I was more than ready to take any seat on a flight to get away from America and get started on the journey that I had always imagined.

CHAPTER 2

Journey to the Holy Land

After the disappointing chain of events before my departure, I was finally able to relax during my sixteen hours of travel time. At this point, I was not even concerned about anything going wrong, just as long as it did not go wrong in America! The in-flight service was not anything to remember, and I did not expect much, taking a small airline. After landing at the Ben Gurion airport, I was not really sure what to expect from Israel. I had spent my whole life reading stories about this place and how it was Jesus' homeland, but there has been a long time in between. Prior to arriving, I initially assumed that Israel would be the holiest of places, and it would be like visiting heaven. I would soon learn that taking new trips can really expose your miscalculations about a certain area.

The "100% Holy Land" idea quickly faded when I arrived at the airport and observed that it was just like any other airport, and the people seemed no different than anywhere else I had been. The interior of the Ben Gurion airport is well designed, and I was surprised to see so many English signs and messages posted. I was still aware that Americans and British people probably travel the most, so the amount of visible English may be tied into that. Even so, for the most part, the Hebrew language was still largely used. Of course, the directing signs were written in Hebrew, but the huge engraved messages in the walls were also in Hebrew. I suppose that was to magnify the "temple feeling" from biblical times, but it was a bit of a culture shock for me, because Christianity in the US has been so Americanized that sometimes I forget that the prophets weren't speaking English. This small change in language highlights one of the main reasons I came to Israel anyway, to learn about the culture of the actual biblical land. The Hebrew writing served as a great first lesson.

I was not oblivious to the fact that Israel is usually a danger zone, and that they may be suspicious of anyone traveling there. I expected to be held for a while and checked thoroughly before being released into the city. I was not sure if they came across "Yes, I'm a Black man from America traveling the world by myself, and I wanted to start in Israel" frequently, so I understood if they held me. Surprisingly, getting past customs was fairly easy, without many questions. I was so hyped up to go to Israel that hadn't looked up where my hotel was, how to get there, and how much the transportation might cost. Over time, I've developed a habit of waiting until I get to the airport, then exploring the transportation option that makes the most sense.

This time, I decided I would take a taxi because I had some heavy bags, and did not have the energy to drag them on a train or bus. The first hour of my Israel trip was incredibly eye-opening, because I saw something I had not expected. I had no expectations when it came to seeing people of color from Israel that spoke Hebrew. The idea hadn't even crossed my mind that people as dark as me, possibly sharing the same hip hop musical interests as myself, could live in Israel. As I said before, you never realize how much your expectations are based on misinformed assumptions until you actually travel to the destination and see for yourself. When I arrived at the taxi stop, I saw two young ladies directing the potential taxi passengers and, to my amazement, they both looked like they could have come from my neighborhood back home. I'm not the type of person to Google "What type of people am I going to find in this particular city," and it does not really cross my mind. I'm usually caught up in the landmarks and monuments that I plan on seeing when I arrive. However, when I saw those young ladies and heard that they spoke Hebrew and English, it changed my thinking a great deal.

Once I made it into the taxi, I expected a quiet ride to my hotel while I enjoyed the view of the countryside in Israel. For me, it made sense to stay in a city outside of Tel Aviv for the first day so I could get an idea of different parts of the area. Since I had no idea where I was going, I gave the city and hotel name to the driver, not expecting much else from him. He struck up a conversation, asking where I was from and why I had come to Israel. After I explained my background, he told me of all the great things Tel Aviv had to offer. The taxi driver, who was most likely in his thirties, covered everything from the landmarks to clubs to tips about the women. Imagine traveling to the "Holy land" and having your first conversation be about partying. Talk about an eye-opener! I'm positive that it was something that God wanted me to see, however, so I could alter my expectations for the future.

I stayed in Herzliya, a beautiful beach town right outside of Tel Aviv, before entering the capital city. The hotel was not far from the beach boardwalk, so a nice stroll was welcome at any time. When I walked to the beach in Herzliya, there was a strong sense of calmness in the air. Although the town is located right by the water, the temperature was intensely hot and not humid at all. The sun was present, there was not much wind, and I did not feel the "rat race" atmosphere that America often has. Herzliya did appear to be an affluent suburb of some sort, but the beach was populated with available hotels and restaurants. After my trip to the beach, I began my usual promenade to see if I could find a restaurant to my liking. I passed a small restaurant called Tandoori and decided to enter, because the setup and design was tastefully done. I chose the Lamb Biryani, and it was far more authentic than I expected. Unfortunately, I was also not expecting the portion to be so heavy, and I was forced to walk around the city for a bit until the size of my dinner was finally in agreeance with my stomach. My first day in Israel was rather tranquil, but I planned for things to pick up once I made my way to Tel Aviv the next day.

In my opinion, the city of Tel Aviv is like Paris, except by a beach. The taxi ride to my Tel Aviv apartment allowed me to gain an understanding of the neighborhoods near the sea. I still had the "Holy Land" idea chiseled into my mind, so it surprised me that much of the city was modernized. The city had a great vibe and culture to it, and I recognized this even before I saw the beach. One thing that may bother Americans when they travel to older cities is that the buildings may be considered below their standards.

Many of us are used to seeing bright lights and everything shiny when we travel, but some areas in cities do not really focus on that luxury. Sometimes the buildings may not have the perfect stucco, or the plumbing may smell horrible because it's not up to code. These are things that you may need to consider if you are going to travel to a city and aren't able to spend top dollar to stay in the most luxurious hotel there.

As I'll continually reiterate, I travel to see the country and the people, not a hotel room, so every trip isn't always regal and luxurious. My apartment was not a dungeon, but it was not a place where I was planning to stage my Instagram photos. Immediately after dropping my bags in my room, I wanted to return to the street that my taxi had driven down on the way to the apartment. The street had lots of stores that were selling arts and crafts that expressed the region's culture. I was also a few blocks from the beach, so it was also possible to take a detour to the boardwalk on the way back. My walk through Tel-Aviv reminded me of Paris, because walking through the local park had the same feeling of a beautiful day along the Seine. The closer I got to the beach, the more it felt like this could be a coastal city in France. Interestingly enough, I also happened to hear a surprising amount of people speaking French in the area where I was staying. Everything considered, I found this section of Tel-Aviv to be very relaxing and far from a tourist trap.

Since I'm from Philadelphia, I'm not used to living so close to a peaceful beach with clear water. My family was not the type to pack up and go to the shore for a weekend, so the beach was not something I frequented growing up. (I do not feel like my Miami trips count, because the beach was just a bonus to the South Beach vibe.) As such, staying only a block from the beach in Tel Aviv, I deemed it necessary to walk on the boardwalk every day throughout my time in the city. Even when I do travel to beaches, I've never had the desire to lay on the beach and just soak in the vacation. A nice walk on the boardwalk or through the city is usually sufficient for the therapy part of my vacations. I never learned how beneficial a nice walk could be until I went abroad and saw the parks in Paris. Philadelphia has a number of parks, but I seldom had the desire to walk around and enjoy the fresh air. For this reason, I understand why it's necessary to travel and see different places, because it might help you add something positive to your everyday life. Being in a foreign setting, your mind comprehends that you are in uncharted territory, so it's acceptable to try something different.

My main reason for taking a trip to Israel was to see Jerusalem—maybe the other famous biblical cities as well, but primarily Jerusalem. Tel Aviv was just a city that was easy to fly into, and one that I had been previously told about by a native. When I was working with my last employer at a bank, I met a client who came from Israel and I had shared my desire to travel there. He told me a little about Tel Aviv and what to expect, also suggesting that it may be too hot to go in the summer. One interesting thing that he said was that his real estate success in the US would be a million times more difficult in Israel. He explained that the simple process of getting a building permit for construction in the USA could possibly take ten years in Israel. That little bit of information gave me peace as I was dealing with "permit patience" for my own properties in Philly at the time.

After experiencing Tel Aviv, I was ready to see Jerusalem and take in the historic atmosphere. A couple of natives explained how easy it was to take a bus there and where I needed to go to get to the bus stop. The walk from the beach to the central city bus stop was not that far, so I figured I would skip the local bus. Journeying through the different neighborhoods felt like a walk through any other big city. The closer I got to the central city, the more it began to feel like a neighborhood in New York City. I did not know what type of buses to expect when I arrived at the transportation stop to Jerusalem, but they were quality charter buses, and boarding was a fairly smooth process. I do not recall the exact price at the time, but it was fairly inexpensive to go to any of the biblically relevant cities in Israel. The bus was packed, and it was obvious that the bus operators were trying to get as much money as they could per ride. There were even people sitting in the aisles and on the back stairs.

The extreme heat that day only added to the discomfort on the bus, because the air conditioning was not working. In America, operating in this condition would have been impossible, as most passengers would have complained on several travel review websites. Even though it was extremely hot, I managed to catch the scenery of the countryside. Israel is a beautiful place outside of the big cities, and I saw a few towns built along hills that overlooked an amazing view. The ride was fairly smooth for a while, but as we got closer to Jerusalem, traffic became congested. The hot and humid conditions made the congestion even worse, and by the time we arrived, I had either fallen asleep or had passed out—I can't remember.

I'm not sure what I was expecting, but the bus station in Jerusalem was under a bridge somewhere, and my initial impression was that it looked like a grimy street that hadn't been cleaned in a while.

Once I wandered around to the market side of the station, things brightened up a bit, and appeared to be more polished. This would be an all-day trip, so I figured walking would allow me to slow down and really appreciate what I was passing. The new tramrail appeared to be the only thing that took away from the ancient feel of the city. While walking along the tramway to reach the Tower of David, I noticed that the strip was mostly for tourists. There were several residential areas, but as I continued walking, I saw more franchised clothing and electronic stores. I was a bit amazed to see the same sneaker stores that we have in the US, but I guess that's my ignorance of thinking certain countries cannot be up to date on fashion. As I got closer to the Tower of David, the small town theme returned with more restaurants and mom and pop shops.

When I first gazed at the Tower of David, it was apparent that the Israelis had gone to great lengths to preserve it, and even welcomed tourists to come visit. I only knew that the Tower of David was relevant to the Bible based on the name alone. Many of the Bible lessons that I learned in Sunday school had to do with King David and his trials and tribulations. America has a large population of Christians, but there are no landmarks that you can refer to in the US that are identified in the Bible. It was an incredible sight to finally see a landmark that was present during biblical times. I researched to see if there was any mention of the Tower of David in the Bible. One verse I found was in Song of Solomon, when Solomon was admiring his bride's beauty:

"Your neck is like the tower of David, built with courses of stone; on it hang a thousand shields, all of them shields of warriors." - Solomon 4:4 NIV

There are other scriptures in the Bible where the Tower of David might be referred to, but in those verses it's not actually called by its name. It is believed to have been fortified by King Hezekiah to protect the area from any invasions. Over the years, the area has gone through some changes, as different empires have passed through the land. The Romans used the Tower of David as a fort for their troops when they destroyed the city of Jerusalem. The Arabs also renovated the tower during their conquest in the 7th century.

I'm not sure how much renovation the zone had gone through over the years, but the Tower was well constructed and seemed like a maze due to its complicated defensive design. The designs of the stones are unique, and it's easy to tell that the site was carefully crafted. I got so caught up in the architecture that I forgot that this site was only built for military purposes and not to be solely aesthetically pleasing. Whatever the case, the Tower of David seems to be secure as a tourist attraction and a place of peace. I was not able to go to the top of the Tower, as it was closed at the time, but the surrounding view was still fascinating.

While I stood in astonishment of the structure, I was startled back into the 21st century. A young cashier was playing one of the most popular songs at the time— "Panda," by Desiigner— just thirty feet away from the Tower of David. For me, that's more shocking than hearing rap music being played at my church back home in the States. But, I remembered I was here to learn about another area, and that showed me how much an influence music has. The noise did not tone down much from there, as most of the streets and alleyways nearby were full of conversations and music from the owners of small shops selling clothes and handmade crafts. The marketplace was within the walls of the fort, so it was like walking down a very narrow hallway with the shops lined together. I continued to walk and look at the many shops selling crafts that might cost a fortune in the States, but which were reasonably priced in Israel. There were also a few shops whose main purpose was to grab the attention of American impulse buyers. There were tons of T-shirts and knick-knacks with your favorite team screen-printed in Hebrew. It seems pretty cheesy and obviously fake, but I cannot lie, they sold me on a Hebrew Philadelphia Phillies shirt.

I'm not very skilled in buying tourism gifts for the women in my family, but one of the premier shops had an exceptional selection of scarves and hand-knit linens. The scarves that caught my eye had a wool-like texture, and their high value was evident. The fabrics were so authentic and high quality that you could tell this was not an ordinary shop. All the small shops were filled to the top with precious valuables, but each individual craft was sophisticated enough to catch your eye. Without a Target or Walmart in sight, quality fabrics and creativity seemed to be the norm in Israel. I figured I would buy a few things from the shops but also pace my spending, because I was sure that there were a lot more interesting souvenirs still waiting in the places ahead. You always want to stop and look in each shop, and each owner is usually at the door enticing you to come in. The coercing is a bit of a turnoff for me, because the quality of products that show in your store should speak for themselves, as was the case in a majority of the market.

A cultural aspect that stood out to me was the interaction between the shop owners, regardless of their background. For those who aren't familiar with the geography of Israel, Jerusalem lies near the border of Israel and Palestine. So, of course, there is a mix of cultures at this specific area. While I was walking through the market, I could hear Hebrew, but also Arabic. The interactions between the different beliefs and cultures were cordial and peaceful. That may sound like a strange observation to natives of Israel, but in the past, I've only heard about the tensions between the two countries and how they cannot get along. It was very encouraging and enlightening to see these people from the different sides interacting with each other as friends. That's just my observation. If they were to come to America, they could possibly say the same thing about some of the groups that are alleged to be at odds.

The shop owners all appeared to be relaxed and easygoing, outside of when they really wanted to make a sale. It's an interesting mentality for them to have, just for the fact that they spend a good amount of their week in a narrow alley away from sunlight. They most likely go through the same routines and types of interactions every day, but you can still feel their sense of pride. This was the first country on my long journey, so Israel was where I first attempted to speak more with the shop owners and learn more about their way of life. There's a lot to be learned from the natives, and you can earn jewels of wisdom by simply asking questions. Whatever their background, there was usually a strong sense of pride and patriotism for their country, and they were more than glad to share about their countries' cultural history and/or current economic problems.

The path through the markets leads to the Western Wall, where you basically reach the summit of the journey. There are many turns and steps as you traverse down the fort, and it starts to become a quest to see when you'll find the entrance of the Western Wall. It did not bother me initially about how far down I was walking, but I began to get a sour taste when I thought about having to take this same walk back up the steps. This may be called the Holy Land, but the steps aren't made of marble or designed to look like a luxurious palace in heaven. The path was nothing more than a mixture of cement and dirt steps that formed rather lengthy planks. I cannot imagine the design and structure of the market being much different from how it was constructed at its beginning.

As I was ready to enter the gates to the Western Wall, I was not sure what to expect because I had not done any research, and I hadn't learned about it in school. I made my way through the entrance, where there were a few guards clustered around an old metal detector, making sure people did not bring contraband in. The moment I walked into this small passage way, I began to feel a new atmosphere that I still can't explain. It's difficult to even try to explain, because of course there was noise from the great amount of people present, but I just remember the calmness in the air. It's without a doubt a tourist landmark in Israel, but it did not feel that way, with all the people just enjoying the sun and the openness of the venue. While I walked down the main stairs, I looked to my right and behind the mass of people relaxing and talking, I could see the countryside. It all appeared to be like a historic scene from a movie, the way the patch of land was untouched, peaceful, and, yes, holy.

As I looked at the historic site, I observed a great deal of people praying against a wall. The scene reminded me of some of the videos that I had seen of people praying in Mecca. Not to say that either site is more sacred or holier, but the wall is far smaller than the praying area in Mecca. The space is like a small section on the side of a building where people can go to pray individually, and I believe you can also touch the wall. I would not classify it as a heavy culture shock, but the experience was different, because when I think of prayer, I think of silence and reverence. But here, there was a small place of peace and prayer, directly next to a giant family reunion type of atmosphere. I do not know many places in

America that are devoted to prayer like this. but it's also surrounded by tons of people casually talking and enjoying the day. I wanted to be as respectful as I could, knowing that this was actually a place of prayer, and some people might find this to be a very serious moment. At the same time, many people there were in a great mood, and the serious spirit was not as present.

From my personal perspective, I felt like my arrival at the Western Wall was telling me that I had made it to a checkpoint in my life. Even beyond the struggles just to make the trip happen, I had worked through many difficulties at my last job and much earlier. I now felt free, as I was away from America and traveling on my own to experience something different. The first thing I could compare it to was when Malcolm X said that the first time he felt like a complete human being standing before God was when he went to Mecca. That was the first time I had that feeling, standing in the skyscraper-less hills of Israel. I had listened to God and He had led me to a place that many people will never have the chance to travel. From there, I began to understand that this trip was more than just a getaway. That checkpoint made me understand that this trip had to be bigger than me, and there had to be some sort of positive result that came from it, other than my peace of mind.

After recovering from my state of shock, I was able to fully appreciate the situation and finally just blend in with everyone, breathing in this day of peace. I honestly wanted to go pray at the wall with the others, but I was slightly intimidated. The way people prayed was much like the fashion in which my Muslim friends pray, kneeling and bowing in a sort of rhythm and cadence. I did not have a problem with what religion was at the wall, but I'm just not used to that type of prayer—especially around a bunch of other people. Again, there was no one present at the wall with a "holier than thou" attitude, so I never felt any pressure to appear to be a saint. But I figured I would say my small prayer standing at a distance, and that would be sufficient. I spent the rest of my time at the Western Wall sitting off to the side and just enjoying the view of the hills. It was therapeutic, but I was also mentally preparing myself to walk back up all of those steps.

As I made my way back to the Tel Aviv bus, I focused on the sights of Jerusalem much more, as the anticipation I'd felt as I headed to the Tower of David was gone. The open roads and palm trees really make Jerusalem a great place to visit. I did not get to see the entire culture of the city because I never completely ventured off of the tourist trail from the bus station to the Tower of David, but it's still very easy to get an idea of its personality. The sun was setting during my walk back to the station and proved to be a great cap to my Jerusalem journey. All I could hope for was a smooth ride back to Tel Aviv with a bus that was not at or over its full capacity. Fortunately, the bus was basically empty, and the ride back was a breeze through the night in Israel. My last hurdle before the night was over was to find some food while I walked downtown. I never stopped to eat in Jerusalem because I feared missing the last bus to Tel Aviv.

The night journey from the bus station to downtown Tel Aviv was a small adventure as I walked through major commercial construction and empty boulevards. It wasn't the safest decision, but my hunger pushed me to hope that I would walk by a nice restaurant at some point. After I walked aimlessly around downtown Tel Aviv, I came across a building that looked like it had a mall inside. The mall looked like an exact duplicate of the shopping centers you would find back in the States. I was so hungry at this point that any food court cuisine would've been perfectly fine. At this stage in my life, I do not even look at the food courts in malls because my body will not agree with anything on their menus. However, the selection of restaurants in the Tel Aviv food court was rather respectable. I was able to find a franchise with a clean meal that consisted of vegetable rice and baked chicken. The other options in the food court weren't far off from slightly healthier food you might find in America.

I was thoroughly pleased with my trip to Israel, and now had my eyes set on Egypt. I knew Israel was a safety risk to travel to, and there might be a thorough review of my credentials coming into the country. Nonetheless, I was not expecting to be held up and interrogated as I left the country. I went through a small kiosk that served as a checkpoint to get into what appeared to be a small airport entrance. The agent looked at me and my passport over and over and decided to look further into my profile and also to have someone else interrogate me. In his defense, I got my passport in 2007 and it was now 2016, and the picture was well outdated, as I have a full beard now. It was not a long and drawn out process (mainly because I'm not a terrorist or spy), but I was concerned that I might miss my flight because some agent thought I was up to something. It's a sad reality, but I do not think many races around the world expect young Blacks from America to do much traveling. We're rarely seen, so it sparks the curiosity of other races when they see us abroad.

CHAPTER 3

Chaos in Cairo

One of the main factors that fuels my desire to travel to new places is that I usually do not know what to expect from different countries. Even with all the documentaries on television and social media photos from your friends, you still may not be able to understand a place until you go there for yourself. Most people expected the political unrest in Cairo, Egypt, to scare me away from traveling there, but I honestly did not think that visiting the pyramids for a day or two would be so dangerous. I understand that the safety warnings are in place to help travelers avoid any conflict or bodily harm, but I honestly think situations can sometimes be exaggerated. Those same videos that are shown of protests, with fires and tear gas being thrown, can and do happen in "the good ol'" USA, so I do not think it's something that should be heavily feared. Even when people think about coming to Philadelphia, some are aware of our homicide problems and think that we have shootouts in every neighborhood from sunup to sundown. This is simply because that's the way the media makes it seem sometimes. Whatever the case, I was not going to let civil unrest deter me from getting to Egypt.

After I boarded the plane and the flight took off, it was far too late to change my mind—not that I was having those thoughts anyway. I consider Israel to be a part of Africa, but in "society's" view, Egypt was my first official visit to the continent. I really was not sure of the reception that I would receive as an American, but the hosts took care of me as soon as I stepped off the plane. After paying my visa fees, or "cover charge," as I like to call it, I was immediately met by an Egyptian man claiming to be an official who would help me get where I needed to go. As a person who grew up in the city of Philadelphia, the last thing I do is trust anybody who comes up to me saying that they want to help me. Making poor choices like that in my hometown can get you robbed, or even worse, lead to you losing your life. The gentleman flashed credentials that appeared to be legit, and the vibe that I got from him did not say "thief," so I allowed him to show me the way to the baggage claim.

He said he would help me with my bags and direct me to the proper taxi to get me to my hotel. When traveling, this is a key point in your trip, because as you will learn in this book, the taxi is where some locals might take advantage of your lack of knowledge of your whereabouts. Most tourists are also looking for any help they can get, simply because they are fatigued from their flight. I do not know how, but as soon as you walk through customs, they can smell the lack of travel experience on you, and you appear as fresh meat. The best idea is to take your time and appear to be relaxed and unrushed, even if you aren't.

Once the man realized I was an American, he decided to strike up a conversation that caught me off guard. The gentleman told me that he admired the democracy that we have in America and wished that his country had the same. This was actually before the

2016 US presidential election and the extreme political views that developed in 2017. So he was probably referring to seeing Barack Obama as president. At any other time, I would have laughed his comment off as sarcasm, but you could hear the admiration in his voice. The media had really sold him on America, and he probably was not aware of all the serious issues we have. I simply told him, "It's not all what it seems," and that he was probably just seeing what the American media wanted him to see. I wonder what that same gentleman thinks about America after 2017.

The sun and the dry heat hit me in the face as soon as I exited the airport, before I could even focus on how I was going to get to my hotel. Cairo International Airport is predictably situated in a spacious region of open desert. The day I arrived, the Egyptian sky was reminiscent of a sun-centered postcard. Now that I had my bags, the official took me to a taxi that would take me to my hotel for a reasonable price. I'm not a violent person by any means, but I was prepared to fight just in case this was a set-up. Some may think I'm joking, but no, you really have to watch your back when you are traveling alone. Nonetheless, that concern for my life quickly transitioned once the taxi ride started and we got onto the freeway. The first five minutes away from the Cairo airport is a beautiful sight, with untouched sand and big signs, but it changed once we hit traffic. I soon realized that driving in Africa is an experience that's completely different from anything you might experience in America—even New York City.

We were on a fairly big highway with a view of downtown Cairo to one side and residential buildings to the other side. I do not remember any traffic lines painted at all, and I'm not sure they would have mattered anyway. It felt like I was in a NASCAR race, but everybody was honking their horns constantly. Based on my observations of the poor conditions of many cars, I doubt there are any yearly inspections in Egypt. It seems that the only thing that matters when it comes to cars is that you can get it running and it can get to your destination. My taxi driver was driving with a technique that I hadn't seen before. Whenever he saw two cars that were a few inches apart, he would honk his horn, so they could move and let him through. There were about ten other cars using the same method in a group of about thirty-five altogether. Aside from the "hooptis" and barely running cars, there were carpool vans (which usually didn't have doors on the back) with passengers just fitting themselves wherever they could. My eyes constantly scanned the madness around the car as we weaved in and out of traffic. One good thing about our speed, however, was that we were going fast enough to cancel out the intense desert heat and gas fumes discharging from the old cars. Despite all of this chaos, there were still people on the side of the road looking to get a ride for a small fee, or even for free if they could. The wildest thing I saw while on the freeway was a man on a scooter with his daughter riding on his lap steering along with him amongst this mad dash. I'd like to make you feel better and say they had helmets on, but that would be a lie. I think his young son was holding on behind him, but I honestly cannot remember. Maybe I don't want to.

I chose a hotel that was right next to the Great Pyramids of Giza so I would not have to travel that far when I got there. If I had done my proper research, I would have known that Giza is a separate city and you have to travel through all of Cairo to get there. The drive was far, but it allowed me to get an idea of the living conditions in the city. The highway is wide for both directions of traffic, but the highway shoulders are littered with significant amounts of trash. The trash seemed endless, and I wondered why it was difficult to collect and dispose of it somewhere. I know I've been spoiled by my American life, where our city governments spend hours and tons of tax dollars to keep highways clean and clear of potholes, but I expected there to be more effort towards cleaning the roads.

The other impression of Cairo that initially bothered me was the quality of the residential buildings that were being built alongside the highway. The majority of the buildings seemed to be the shoddiest kind of work you could find, and most of them looked like unfinished new construction. I saw countless buildings with subpar masonry work that looked like it would take a miracle to have corrected. These construction blunders were everywhere throughout the ride, and I wondered what the reason could be. It's an eyesore for any city, in any country, but we're actually talking about a place where The Great Pyramids of Giza were built. The finest crafts and artifacts from centuries ago can be found here in Egypt. I was stunned to see such poorly constructed apartment buildings.

At this point, I did not know what to expect from my hotel, but I was just hoping to make it to the Pyramids before they closed. When I arrived at my hotel, I could see the Pyramids, and I was even closer than I had thought. My taxi driver tried to finesse me for more money, but I was too focused on getting checked in and getting to Pyramids before sundown. It was a pretty intimidating set-up, complete with a metal detector, to get into the hotel, but it was a smooth check-in for the most part. The hotel had a burgundy and gold theme that you might find in a 70's disco movie, but it was clean, so I did not really care about the design. It was close to closing time, but I knew I still had a small chance of getting into the Pyramids, so I ran down to yell for another taxi.

I was instructed by the airport official to only take a certain official taxi that the government had record of, because they get in serious trouble if anything happens to you. I followed directions and found the first government taxi that came my way. From here, the journey to seeing the Pyramids officially became a quest with my second taxi driver. My driver took me to the gate, where you are pretty much on your own if you did not come with a tour or had plans set up already. Even before I got out of the car to walk up, there was a guy talking to me from the outside of the car, saying he could help me and that he would give me directions. This guy had no credentials, and his eyes were lit up because he could tell that I did not know where I was going or what I was doing. I've forgotten his name, but it was clear from the start that he had an agenda that had was different than mine. What that agenda was, I'm not really clear on, other than he wanted money. I got out of the car and realized at the last second that I had left my phone on the seat, a move that would have been catastrophic if I hadn't checked. At this point, everything just started happening so fast, and it was like one of those points in the basketball game where you need to take a timeout to regroup. Multiple "guides" were telling me they could help me, but the officials directing traffic were saying that I couldn't enter this way, but through another gate.

I quickly flagged down another cab and asked him to take me to the other gate, where I could gain entrance into the Pyramids. This cab driver had a different angle, which was to earn money through flattery. I told him I was from America and he immediately went into a loud lecture about how Black Americans are "the original man." I was not sure if he was serious, but I found it interesting that someone from a different culture could strongly believe that about my people. He wasn't trying to overpraise, but I could sense that he was looking for a generous tip. Whatever the case, he had his own driving agenda, and he started by saying that he could help me get into the Pyramids by taking his own route. I knew this was the wrong taxi to take, and I soon had to get out of the car. He drove me to a back alley and said that If I gave him and his friend some more money, he could get me the "special tour." Fortunately, God blessed me with an opportunity to be raised in Philadelphia, and I'm familiar with "special tours in back alleys." So I had to switch out of tourist mode and back to Philly mode. I looked him dead in the face and told him to take me to the back gate where the tourists are, and I did not even have to mention that there would be a problem if he did not.

After arriving at the back gate, I was greeted by even hungrier and younger "guides" willing to "help" me on my journey. It was becoming annoying, so I began to beg them to leave me alone as I tried to figure out my next move. It was clear that I was not going to make it inside the Pyramids today, so I was going to have to hit all three spots I wanted to see in Cairo the next day before my evening flight. I did, however, learn a lesson at the back gate about how to handle the annoying "guides." Two West African men were standing by the gate, looking extremely calm as they discreetly waved off anybody looking for a sale. I figured I would take this approach from now on, since my American plan hadn't worked too well.

My cab ride back to the hotel was eye-opening because we went through a small residential section to get there, and it showed the conditions that some of the people live in. This was my first trip to Africa, so it was difficult to get used to the social norms. It's clear that the money does not flow throughout the different classes, and earning income is difficult on the streets, so people just make it how they can. Even around the Pyramids, a lot of the buildings are completely broken up, with no real plans in place to reconstruct them. The streets were totally packed with people walking the streets, either with young guys hanging out or selling something, or young and elderly ladies walking to the store or to work. The traffic and lack of organization made it seem even more chaotic. The entire time there, it seemed like there were tons of cars on the road, and even with four to five people in a car, there was always traffic. Interestingly, I observed that although it seemed like it was an "every man for himself" environment, there appeared to be a great deal of teamwork in Egypt. Whether it was with the officials and the taxi drivers, or the guys in the streets working together. It seemed that they were more willing to work from the bottom together to earn some money or build something as a team.

After failing to achieve my goal of visiting the Pyramids, I immediately started searching for food, hoping to taste some of the Egyptian cuisine that I had heard about over the years. I had looked up some restaurants online that I could possibly walk to, like I did in Paris and Italy. My taxi driver told me that this would be a poor decision, because I would promptly be beaten and have my things taken by the locals. Part of me took that as a marketing ploy for him to get more money, but I respected his advice. I usually can get a sense if there's a place that I shouldn't be walking because danger is imminent, but I did not sense that in this section of Giza. However, I figured I would listen because it had already been too eventful of a day, and I did not want to encounter more drama. Luckily, my hotel had a buffet that night, based on a mixture of Egyptian and Mediterranean cuisine.

The food was okay, but I was more focused on the fact that I was eating my dinner outside with the Great Pyramids of Giza in the background. The temperature and humidity seemed to be pretty steady throughout the day, so when the sun went down, my dinner outside was rather therapeutic. The only drawback was the amount of bugs, mainly mosquitoes, that came to bother me while I was outside. I thought of a strategy for the next day during dinner, thinking of the most time-efficient way to see everything. My intention for the next day was to go through the Pyramids tour and then head downtown to go to the Egyptian Museum. I knew I had to get a sufficient amount of sleep in order to have the energy for what was going to be undoubtedly be long day. There was no way for me to estimate the time it would take to get around the Pyramids and then head downtown, but I knew I had an evening flight, and I had to be done by 4:30 PM. I hung out in the hotel lobby a little while before heading back to my room, but the decor did not provide much to look at, and the wi-fi was not strong at all. If the mosquitoes weren't so terrible, I would have sat out on the hotel room's deck and just gazed at the Pyramids. The day I had been dreaming about as a kid was just hours away. Even though it was difficult, I found a way to sleep through the anxiety.

CHAPTER 4

The Great Pyramids of Giza

I woke up early, skipped breakfast, and left the hotel dressed to
look as little like a tourist as I could. I felt like a seasoned traveler,
so I took the cab to the exact destination I needed to go and was
even able to negotiate a good fare. I arrived at the gate, and
although it was only a short wait until the security check to see this
great world wonder, it seemed like an eternity. I was, however, able
to loosen up after the security checkpoint agent joked with me by
asking if I had a bomb. I'm not sure if that's an occasional joke he
makes, or if that's how anxious I looked trying to get through the
line.

Breezing through the checkpoint, which is in a small hut, I
stepped out. As I saw the giant sun peeking over the Pyramids, I
felt like I had finally finished a quest. I couldn't have asked for a
better day of weather, with a clear sky and the sun beaming down
on the Egyptian sand. I stood in awe for about a minute before
finally snapping back to life and began walking towards the first
pyramid. At first, the world around me was silent as I examined all
of the pyramids' intricate details, but yells coming from random
Egyptian men walking towards me interrupted the peace. They
wanted me to take a camel ride or let them guide me around the
pyramids. I really wanted to enjoy this by myself, so I declined

continuously. Once you get inside the pyramid grounds, the unofficial guides and salesmen are less aggressive, but far more strategic, to say the least.

After realizing that the locals could smell the American on me, I decided to switch my demeanor, using what little French I knew and walking around as a Francophone from Africa. I was very calm with how I walked and politely declined in French using minimal words. That only worked a little bit, as these gentlemen happened to be fluent in French as well. I honestly think these guys that offer to help for a fee might know at least six or seven languages. I watched them approach me, then approach other people from different countries, and the language barrier seems to be non-existent. They do not care what language you speak, as long as you have a widely accepted currency!

As I walked closer to the first pyramid, I was amazed at how gigantic the bricks are that make up the pyramids. I then understood why people have a hard time thinking that the pyramids could be real or even made by humans. We live in such lazy and lethargic times that it's almost unfathomable that such a structure could be put together only using math, science, and combined manpower. The difficulty of the architecture alone makes it seem impossible, and the fact that the Egyptians had no machines strengthens that thought. When I went over to the Museum of Cairo later in the day, I was able to understand the level of their detail once I looked at the smaller artifacts.

The first giant pyramid had an entrance where you could see the inside, but I was not really ready for that type of adventure at such an early part of the day. I decided I would tour the area first and go inside the pyramid later, if I was in the mood. I guess I had been influenced by the visions of the American land developers where the stadiums are directly in the middle of the city or not far off. I was amazed at the actual size of the area around the pyramids and how the individual pyramids had been randomly placed throughout the allotted space. I later learned that the ancient Egyptian developers had to have done extensive calculations to align the corners of the pyramids with the cardinal points: North, South, East, West. Some pyramids were giant in size and others low to the ground, or a size in between, but all seemed to have their own design and layout on the inside.

Initially, I was unsure about my method of tourism, because there were so many people who took the tour buses or had a camel carry them around to the various pyramids. It did not seem like a far walk between the pyramids because of their visibility, but they turned out to be a nice twenty minute walk from each other. However, I had so much energy and eagerness to walk the whole desert that it did not matter in terms of stamina—although maybe for safety. A handful of people had the same idea as me of walking through the pyramids on their own on roughly laid-out walkways and experiencing the details of the site for themselves. With the help of some of these people, I was able to create some of the pictures I had envisioned of myself at the Pyramids for years. Perhaps it was better this way, because if I had had one of my friends there, they would have gotten tired of my need for tons of picture angles.

As I walked through the grounds, I truly felt that this was an adventure that everyone should be able to go on at least once in their lives, to see some sort of greatness from the past. I thought of the many days in grade school where I felt my time was wasted learning about guys like Christopher Columbus, who I feel gets more credit than he deserves for just traveling. Many people would say that Egypt is the most well-known country in Africa, but somehow, I never learned much about the country in school. In all my years of grade school, I do not remember much talk about any African empires, history, or places. At the same time, I'm sure anybody can tell you the names of at least one of the three ships that Columbus used. So from that point forth, I knew that I would attempt to educate people about the history of Africa. If anything, I'm sure most people recognize the common designs and monuments of Egypt.

The most iconic Egyptian structure, in my opinion, is the Sphinx, which I had not been able to locate immediately. I was told that it was located a little ways to the left of my location at the time, so I went on a small walk towards the site. If you decide to go to the Great Pyramids of Giza, for safety I recommend that you get a bus or ride to the pyramids. I do admit, though, that it might be a better sightseeing experience if you walk throughout the area. Even by just walking from pyramid to pyramid, I was able to notice all of the small details that it is impossible to notice from the gravel road by which the buses travel. Many tours may drive up to the front and have you go inside the pyramid, but you might not have the time to walk all around and see the small, detailed work that the Egyptians added.

I was able to see what seemed to be small jails that were created and also some smaller buildings that may have housed some of the keepers. The majority of people go to historic places and book tours where they have no real control over the time and/or content they're able to see. As a result, they may have paid $5000 for the prestigious name of the tour and country, but only have gotten a $2000 value. Part of the reason I wrote a book and created BraveVoyage.com was to give people the idea to have an open mind when traveling, and to encourage them to experience more rather than to just be catered to. Many agencies and countries know that most Americans are just looking to be pampered and catered to during their vacations, so they only focus on safety and customer service, but may neglect the experience aspect of the country.

Throughout my pyramid journey, I bumped into several people who wanted to practice their English with me. After spending a month in Paris, I've become used to people wanting to practice their English on me by making small talk. It just so happens that I was traveling during interesting political times, and the only thing people wanted to talk about was Donald Trump or Hillary Clinton. These excursions were before Trump got elected, so it was still a laughing matter and most people just laughed it off as a typical American joke. It was a joke for them, but while traveling, I was still trying to make sense of how this joke was still not over despite all of the looming controversies.

I made my way down to the Sphinx, but I was disappointed to find out that the tour was closed off for the day. I'm not sure if I was given a legitimate reason, but I did not care much, since I was still able to get a great view for my selfie and some professionally angled photos. The Great Sphinx is something that I had to see for myself, because everybody has heard the various reasons for why many people think the nose is not there anymore. Due to the tour being closed, I was not able to locate anyone who looked like they might have an answer. But that issue was small potatoes compared to the view that you can see once you stand in front of the Great Sphinx. Before traveling to Egypt, I was intrigued by the construction of the pyramids alone, but as I walked through the land, I developed an admiration for the creative vision that the leaders had for the area. The opening from the city leading up to the pyramids is visible from the Sphinx's side, and it's obvious how sophisticated the land developers were at that time. The kings and developers of that time had a completely different mindset when creating ideas. After watching many documentaries, I came to understand that the actual goal of the various leaders was for these visions.

From the vantage point of the Great Sphinx, I could see that there were some people going on the camel tours out to the empty desert, but being a solo traveler, there was zero chance I would be experiencing that. In my opinion, it's far too dangerous to travel out to the desert with people you do not know, in an area you are not familiar with. I decided that I would go into at least one of the Pyramids towards the entrance and see what was inside. The smaller pyramid looked like a strain to crawl into, and there were not many people on that side, so I went with the safer, tourist-laden pyramid where there was a big opening. The ticket that I had purchased covered the entrance fee, so it was not a difficult decision. I usually shy away from tourist-heavy areas because the atmosphere becomes artificial and you can lose the sense of the country, but I made an exception for the pyramids.

As I mentioned before, the blocks used to make the Pyramids are gigantic, and climbing up to get to the entrance is slightly intimidating. However, that timidity went away when I saw everyone else doing it easily. I'm not ashamed to admit that I had some fear of walking into a structure that was made thousands of years ago. Idiotic questions begin to pop into my head like, "Is it going collapse while I'm in there?". After a few steps through a narrow path, I looked up and saw steps, lots of steps. Not the kind of steps that you would ascend in your house, but the kind you have to crawl up, staying low the whole time. The opening to the interior steps is very tight and the climbing quickly becomes an intense workout. Without much fresh oxygen, I was easily tired, and I began to sweat profusely. Not knowing what to expect, the continuous ascent felt like an eternity, but it may have only been ten to 15 minutes until I reached the top of the steps.

The top of the steps led to a partially lit room with an empty tomb in the middle. The room was maybe fifteen feet long and ten feet wide, and was far off from the shiny gold pictures you might see in history books. After reaching the room, I spent the first two minutes catching my breath, acting like I was looking at the detail in the walls. There weren't any other parts of the pyramid available to the public, and I'm sure they can't display the precious artifacts that may have been left behind years ago. While I'm sure there was much more to see in the Pyramid, I'm aware that the government has to put some limits on the access to this world wonder. I spent the last minute in the room, mentally preparing myself to get down the stairs without falling all the way to the bottom.

The trip down the pyramid steps proved to be even more of a challenge, since I had to be careful with my footing as I made my way down the steep passageway. I exited the pyramid alive, and I was ready to take my final pictures before heading to the Egyptian museum. Of course, I was met by the local "officials" and street sellers trying to earn a tip. Their greetings were no different from anything I might find at home in Philadelphia, with their random outbursts. The brothers greeted me with labels like "Sudan, Sudan," referring to idea that I looked like I was from Sudan in Africa. To be transparent, it makes me feel welcome when Africans think I'm from any part of Africa. Another gentleman came up to me and said, "You have an Egyptian beard," and gave me a scarf to put on so I could take pictures. After taking many breathtaking pictures in front of the Pyramid, he immediately asked for money, which I had made sure not to carry too much of, in case I lost it. The most common greeting in Africa that a Black American may receive is "my brother." Sometimes it seems a bit patronizing, but at times it's obviously genuine, and other times, a mix of both. After the scarf man, other people approached me in hopes of tips, but I only brought enough for the entrance fee and the cab to and from the pyramids.

It was a race against time as I hurried back to my room to get prepared to head downtown to the Egyptian Museum. I found a cab that could take me downtown and give me a different view of the Cairo-Giza area—away from the pyramids or the highway. Even after a long airport trip and a few cab rides, I still did not feel comfortable with the driving atmosphere in Africa. As we were driving in the cab, the driver shared some history and explained the current situation in Cairo. It took me a few different times to understand what he was saying, but I finally figured out that he was telling me that we were driving across the Nile. My face instantly lit up after hearing that I was driving over a river that I had heard about since my younger days in Sunday school. I obviously hadn't done enough research on the places that I was traveling, but I suppose that it was better, because I was learning about these places naturally, instead of looking at a checklist.

The scene downtown was not much better than what I had seen along the highway, but the open space around the Museum was a stunning view. After standing still and looking around for a few minutes, I honestly believe that the sun shines differently in Africa. Among the business in the street, and the many conversations, the sun still brought a calm to my place in the middle of downtown Cairo. I did not even realize until after I left the country that this was the scene of recent civil unrest. Center City Cairo reminded me of a downtown you might see in any other city, but I suppose that they carved out a nice spot in front of the

Museum for tourists. I was not sure if the military/police presence was a normal thing, or if it had to do with the civil problems, but I did have to show ID and explain that I was there for the Museum. A peach-colored, regal-looking building that shines well in the sun, the Egyptian Museum is possibly the most beautiful building in Cairo. The architecture and the detailed doors are pieces of art in themselves, and they set the tone for what you'll see in the Museum. One great thing about traveling is that it motivates me to go to museums and learn about the culture of the places I'm visiting. Shamefully, I rarely visit any museums when I'm in America, and I'm not really sure of the reason. The Art Museum of Philadelphia is one of the most prestigious museums in America, but I've only visited there a few times since my childhood.

I usually travel for different reasons, whether for the authentic food, landmarks, or to meet new people. The Egyptian Museum was a natural motivation for me, because I've seen so many false images stemming from American ignorance. By growing up in America and only being able to depend on Hollywood's depiction of ancient Egypt, a lot of us fail to receive an authentic view of the country. Even up until now in modern times, movies based in ancient Egypt are being depicted by white people with straight hair, for various reasons. Many say, "Well, it's just Hollywood using the big stars to generate profit and tell a story." However, I know that people believe whatever they see, and consequently take these images for the truth. I hypothesized that a trip to the Egyptian museum, where they hold many of the country's paintings, artifacts, and sculptures, would give me the authentic view of the truth.

Walking in and observing the depth of history, I felt like I had reached a distinguished level of tourism. When I was younger, I figured that the only way I would get to see these artifacts was on a page in a *National Geographic* magazine. I thought that this scenario would only happen in a dream, so it was a very humbling experience. On a trip without any serious time constraints, I would have spent the entire day examining all the cultural details and artifacts, but I was mindful that I had a flight to catch. I had missed one flight already on this journey, and I was not ready to miss another. I was told that there was a special ticket that you needed to have in order to take pictures anywhere in the museum, and indeed it was a higher price. It did not matter, because those officials were mistaken if they thought that I had flown all the way over to Egypt and would not take selfies to show I had been there.

The sculptures and tombs were on the bottom floor, which makes sense, because these were made of gigantic and solid stones. As I viewed them, I saw that the Egyptians had been incredibly detailed in their art, from large shapes to the tiny writing and pictures that you find on these tombs. The information cards beside the art did not give me an idea of how long it took to make the various pieces, but the sophisticated details suggested it took a lengthy amount of time. I find it interesting how technology has obviously advanced immensely since ancient Egypt's rule, but you still cannot find many works of art today that compare to Egyptian work. As I wandered from room to room, I could see that the

Museum was well thought out, as it aided visitors in piecing together the history of Egypt by educating them on different rulers and important figures.

On the second floor, the artifacts told more about the actual life and culture of the people of Egypt. The beds, chairs, and thrones for the rulers were luxurious and well detailed by their designers. One interesting thing about the Egyptians is that they knew how great their empire was and made sure that they documented it by writing hieroglyphics in stone and also making small figures and sculptures to show their lifestyles. In today's time, most of us rather simply take pictures and videos to remember our existence, and it usually stops there. Again, the purpose of this book is not to spoil subsequent trips for others, but to give an idea of how your findings might change your perception of a place. I will not go into great detail about the artifacts and sculptures that I saw, but I will highlight the characteristics that resonated most with me.

The Egyptians were sure to show their excursions in ships, and did so by making small little figures, even if there were fifty to a boat. They were well sculpted and detailed realistically, down to the feet. The most interesting thing about these figures is that the skin color is certainly distinct and consistent. It was either red clay figures or very dark-skinned figures, the color that you might find at a museum in Central Africa. I made sure to turn my wi-fi on to show all my friends on Instagram and Snapchat immediately. I found this media sharing method to be the best way to combat the fair-skinned Egyptian ideology of Hollywood. I figured that gathering proof in person, would be far more effective than just drawing up my own conclusions from home in the US. The figures were the authentic pieces, and their existence could speak for themselves.

One other Egyptian characteristic that stuck with me was that they actually had wigs in those times. The wigs looked to be curly hair, and one had strands of braids sticking out of the back. I was shocked that something that seemed to be newly stylish for Black Americans in the 20th century happened to be here thousands of years before we were even thought of. Many of the pieces of jewelry appear to be the same designs that you might find in a modern store. These ancient pieces tell me that there may be a lot of things that we do today that we did not know originated back in Egypt and/or other places in Africa. We know that many of the things that we perceive as the "new" style may have been fashionable thirty to forty years ago, but it's possible that this process actually started thousands of years in the past.

I wanted to stay longer, but I had to play it safe and return to my hotel to collect my things in order to get ready for my next flight—to Kenya. At this point, the trip was already a success, but I was excited to see a new place in Africa after such an amazing journey in Egypt. I returned to my hotel and was able to get one last look at the Pyramids. Anything terrible could have happened and I probably would not have cared, because the last 24 hours had really been a dream movie that I couldn't have scripted myself. The disappointment I felt on the first day and the anticipation leading up to actually going into the Pyramids all turned out to be worth it.

The only disappointment you might encounter is that Cairo isn't the city for you if you are looking for any history or artifacts from Cleopatra's rule. I attribute that misstep to my lack of research, since I failed to realize that her rule was in Alexandria, and not Cairo. I suppose that it was a good thing, because I now have a reason to return to Egypt and see something new and learn more.

By the time I got into a cab on the way to the airport, I was on the verge of being late for my flight. After seeing the traffic in Cairo, I knew that being on time for my flight was no sure thing at all. Although this was going through my mind, I was calmed by the evening sunset and the Arabian music being played in the streets as we drove through the residential sections. The traffic was backed up at this point, but I was reduced to an interested spectator, just watching the street life in Cairo that really was not far off from what you might find in an American inner-city. I drove by a heated argument between a couple of young guys and a small crowd, and also saw some young ladies walking in between the traffic. Most women appeared to be on their way home from work, and still more small motorcycles with multiple helmetless people on them weaved in and out of traffic as I sat in awe. Several women still sat in front of their small stores, trying to make one last sale before closing up.

After we made it out of the residential section, we crossed into the downtown region and moved towards the highway. The Nile is even more beautiful at night as the lights glisten off of its wide body and make it look like it has no end. As the night got darker, the air grew full of dust and became hard to see through. After twenty minutes or so, it started to get hard for me to breathe through the dust and engine fumes, and I wasn't sure if their side effects of poor vision or the bad taste in my mouth was worse. Once we were through all of the heavy traffic, the dust clouds began to break apart, and the cab driver pointed out some of the government buildings and shared some history on them. The Alabaster Mosque was one of them, and in the skyscape of Cairo, it is a beautiful sight that shines brightly through the dust from afar. All in all, my time in Cairo was a little more than twenty-four hours, but the sights and memories of it will last my lifetime.

CHAPTER 5

Nairobi Nights

Getting through the security checks out of Cairo was a breeze, but I was rushing so much that I did not check to see how long the flight to Kenya would be. I think most Americans perceive Africa's size as much smaller than it actually is. I blame the inaccurate maps that we are usually shown in grade school. The more I traveled in Africa, the more I realized that it is a huge continent, and the US is rather small in comparison. My flights from Philadelphia to Miami averaged out at about three hours, and from Philly to Los Angeles at about five hours. My flight from Cairo to Kenya, which isn't even at the bottom of Africa, was scheduled at just under five hours.

Still on a high from my Egyptian trip, I was overly excited about what new people I would meet and all the new experiences I would have, so a long flight did not bother me. The best flight I could find got me into Kenya at about 3:30 in the morning, which did bother me a little, because I was not sure of the best way to get to the bed & breakfast I had booked. I was extremely tired, so I decided I would handle that problem when I had more energy.

My experience at the Jomo Kenyatta Airport in Kenya further revealed to me that God was directing the order of countries I visited. Egypt had exposed me to a bartering technique that I hadn't experienced before. Of course, we have our typical negotiations in America, where you try to squeeze as much as you can out of a salesman, without giving up much. However, that mindset isn't as common among Americans when traveling to foreign countries because they do not know the official rules. Also, most people want smooth transitions into their vacation destinations, especially when they've just gotten off a long flight. In Africa, it's a totally different culture, because even cab rides are up for negotiations, as well as the services that you would assume to be controlled by the official government. I've always been the type of person that loves to get the most bang for my buck, but I've never seen it practiced as naturally as it is in Africa. Egypt served as my "Bartering 101" course, and I learned how to stand firm when negotiating prices.

When some officials and workers see Americans, they know that they came to spend some money on vacation and might not mind paying for something that they do not necessarily need. My sister told me about her travels to Africa and already let me know that there was going to be a visa charge when I got to customs. I went to the ATM and went through the process of obtaining a visa and preparing to receive my bags from customs. I was so worried about getting a cab and being able to get some rest after a long night that I did not even focus much on the customs process. I spoke with a few people about getting around Africa and learned about some problems that I might run into, but I was not prepared at all for the customs problem I was about to face.

Once I paid for my visa, I was met by a gentleman who identified himself as an official and who wanted to know about the reasons for my trip. I did not find it odd, because it's actually common to get asked questions by any country's customs officials, and every country has a different method of handling the process. The official wanted to know where I was staying, how long, and where I was headed after. I explained everything, and he expressed some problems I might run into with customs and how he might be able to help me with the next official that we were walking towards. I did not pay much attention because I really did not understand what he was trying to get at, and I really just wanted to get some sleep. What I failed to understand is, once the US passport is handed to them, they might be thinking of all the ways to get some money out of you, and the next official was about to get "surgical."

The first official handed my passport to the other, along with a short explanation. The second official looked through the booklet slowly, maybe thinking of how much he was going to bleed out of me. His first question was if I had a laptop or any electronics, of which I had both. At the time I had my laptop and my musical drum machine so I can produce music on my down time. The drum machine is rather large, so the official said that I had to pay tax on it to get through into the country. Whenever I travel, I always try to factor in any possible costs, so any unforeseen costs really stir my brain cells. I was not sure if this was an official tax, which it could have been, but I really wanted to hear a good explanation or at least see where this policy was in writing. The gentleman explained that this was a common tax policy and asked how much I could give.

The bargaining skills that I'd learned in Egypt kicked in instantly, and I just explained my situation to the official. I do not want say that I played victim, but I explained that I came to see Africa and I did not have any extra money to pay for taxes. We went back and forth for about a good half hour and it became clear to him that I was not going to budge. I kept explaining that I had more places to go in Africa and I did not know what expenses were waiting for me there. After I wore him down, he finally said that I was free to go and told me to enjoy my trip. Even though I may have embellished the truth, I felt like I finally passed the test and I was officially accepted into Africa.

The first official, who had initially met me, took me through the customs doors to find a taxi and also to share his observations. I still remember his look of approval as he said in his Kenyan accent, "You did very well back there." He said that he was surprised that I got out of that, and it seemed to me that this is a routine process for foreigners. I did not want to celebrate too much, but they did not know they were talking to somebody who specializes in detecting unnecessary fees, especially when I know I'm right. I was happy that I avoided the so-called "official" electronic tax payment, but to receive the approval of an African official made my Kenyan trip worth it in the first hour.

However, getting through customs was only the first part of my Kenyan initiation. Acquiring a reasonable taxi from the airport at 4:30 AM proved to be the next challenge I would face. Once I got past the officials at the airport, I opened the door to a bunch of "taxi drivers" staring at me with blank faces. The air was just as unwelcoming, with a damp thickness clinging to my skin immediately, and there was not one breeze to break it. These taxi drivers all looked like they were my age or younger and had just left the club. It seemed as if they saw fresh American meat and were ready to charge me up for their big payday. Luckily, the first official steered me in the right direction, where I found the taxi that would get me to my bed & breakfast. The appointed taxi driver appeared to be an honest gentleman, so I did not really fear for my safety at any time. Even so, this was still uncharted territory for me, and we were driving in the dark in a country that I had never been to before. My alertness was still high and I was ready to defend myself if I needed to. When traveling by yourself, you have to realize when you are in a vulnerable position, and you need to have a defensive mindset, even if it may seem that you are being too cautious.

The ride was not too long, but I was more than ready to see my bed and get some rest. The choice to stay in a bed & breakfast instead of a hotel allowed me to see a side of the residential lifestyle in Kenya that I might have not seen otherwise. I've seen gated communities throughout the US and the mansions that sit behind gates, but the layout that I saw in Nairobi was slightly different. We pulled up to a neighborhood that looked like a US southern suburb block lined with houses, but they were all gated individually. The cab driver had to knock on the metal door by the gate and identify the vehicle's occupants in order to gain access to the property. I knew the residential system would most likely be different in

Africa, but I did not think people had to live behind gates with multiple security guards present 24/7. Whatever the case, I was far too tired to care, and I just wanted to see where I was sleeping.

The host checked me in and everything went smoothly, but she let me know that if I wanted to see the safari, 5:00AM (which was the current time) was the best time to go. She explained that the most desired animals, like lions, were usually seen early in the morning, because they search for food at that time and just relax in hiding the rest of the day. That information was key, but unfortunately it was of no use to me, as my eyes were already closing and my brain was just about to shut down. I hadn't booked a departing flight yet, so I had time to stick around Nairobi if I wanted to. I knew Tanzania was my next destination, but I just was not sure how I was going to get there. A plane ride would have been easy, but taking a bus ride around Mt. Kilimanjaro would take my trip beyond a vision that I could imagine. In the meantime, I was focused on getting the best experience out of Kenya and meeting some of the locals.

My room was small, and the only thing that bothered me was that I couldn't open all the windows because mosquitoes might get in. I have to reiterate that during my travel, the media was at the peak of its Zika virus coverage, and everyone was terrified of catching it. Because of this, for the entirety of my trip, my conscience was telling me that I needed to avoid all possibilities of mosquito bites. The room was humid and damp with its windows closed, but I guess those conditions would be better than having to go to the hospital for vaccination shots. I figured I'd get some sleep, then wake up for a Kenyan breakfast and explore my options for traversing through Nairobi.

The breakfast that was provided was healthy and full of fruit, which was what I needed to have enough energy for another eventful day. The compound was spacious and appeared to be a house connected to four separate rooms that were lined up like a motel. As I look back now, I guess I may have benefited more from staying at a hotel downtown somewhere, because I would have been able to experience city life and then go check out the safari when I wanted to get away. Even so, it was still a great and cost-efficient choice to be amongst the locals. Aside from exploring the city life, there were different safari tours to choose from, and I was not sure what type of experience I was looking for.

The safari trip was one of the few things I had researched beforehand, and I'd found out that the various companies had several different tour packages, depending on how brave I was feeling. The extremely expensive trips were the types of rides which I felt were the least safe, so that made a cost-efficient decision easy. Most safari companies even had the option of spending some days in big or small tents, which would also not be possible for me in terms of safety. I decided to talk to someone at the bed & breakfast about what the best option might be. I was told that there was a friend of the establishment who could give me a ride to the local safari at Nairobi National Park, and I could just pay the entrance fare for his car. The driver picked me up and drove me to the safari reserve, which looked like a regular local park from the entrance.

I hadn't looked up this safari, so I did not know what to expect from this reserve specifically. So the experience was going to be thrilling and unpredictable. It had rained a lot in the previous days and there were no cloud breaks in the overcast sky, so the terrain was very muddy. I had initially figured that we would be hopping into one of those high-powered jeeps that you see people driving through the safari on YouTube, but that was not the case. The driver picked me up in an old Toyota Camry, and that's what we drove through the mud with. I was still happy to be driving through on a safari, but the feeling was bittersweet, when I saw everybody else driving in giant SUVs or all-terrain jeeps. On a regular mild or sunny day, the Camry may have been good enough, but since it rained the whole week, many roads were only accessible with the proper vehicle.

Driving through the initial trees, the safari opened up to a wide field full of open grass and shrubbery for the animals. I instantly looked for any lions that might be walking around, but I knew that was not likely after missing the early morning special. At first, it was hard to drive around because the road options were limited and we had to take several detours to get to the main part of the safari trail. It was also difficult to keep the window rolled down because the most annoying flies that buzzed in and outside of the car lived inside the park.

The first thing that stuck out to me was that I could see smoke billowing from what appeared to be a bonfire. I quickly remembered that there was a movement to get rid of all animal poachers, so the Kenyan President would burn elephant tusks to discourage anybody from killing any animals. The news said that this was basically millions of dollars going up in smoke, but, to me, placing a number on the loss takes away from the gravity of the situation. I honestly do not believe that you can put a real value on animal parts. It's one of the unfortunate disadvantages of the authorities not being strong enough to stop poachers in some African regions. People come from all over the world to steal various things from Africa, and it seems that the current law enforcement in place isn't strong enough to control the crimes.

As the driver began to get a handle of the terrain, we went farther into the safari reserve. The animals we saw most commonly were gazelles or similar herbivores that could usually be spotted snacking on some shrubbery. I also saw some deer and a giraffe, but nothing that was so amazing that I'll never forget it. We drove around for maybe an hour and a half and the driver did a great job finding what roads he could with the hope that we would run into a lion. The excitement of driving around looking for those lions was comparable to the wildlife adventure shows on TV that string you along until it's time for the next commercial. The result may not have been what I wanted, but it was still definitely worth it.

After the safari trip, I started looking for anything to eat, and I happened to receive a lesson in the process. My safari driver took me to a mall, which was not too far away, and I walked in by myself to see if I could find somewhere worth dining. I had not been in Africa for more than a few days, so I still was not sure what to expect. When I walked into the little mall, I was shocked that it did not look much different from a mall that you might find in the

US. I'm not sure what I expected to see, but I was surprised when I saw cell phone stores, urban clothing stores, and the usual little pointless kiosks in the middle of the walkway. When I say mall, I'm not referring to the ghetto strip malls you might find in the "hood." This was a clean mall that looked like it couldn't have been built more than ten years ago.

As Americans, I think we really have a misguided understanding of the way of life in Africa. American television shows rarely depict the various ways of life in the vast parts of Africa, so many of us fail to imagine that Africans can live just as we do. Whenever a show takes place in Africa, it's usually set in a resort, or somewhere on the countryside, so we tend to believe that's the only setting out there. There needs to be an effort at some point to show the different ways of life in Africa, so Americans (especially Black Americans) do not believe that there is some huge gap between our ways of life. Even in America, lifestyle in the countryside is far different from inner-city life. If the media focused on one American setting, that's all foreigners would believe existed. The more I traveled in Africa, the more I realized that the media's power can be misused.

I did not find anything that looked appetizing in the food court, and anyone that knows me would say that I would've had the same problem in American food courts. Fast food is something that I might do maybe five times a year. In the end, I decided I would try the Kenyan KFC, simply for the fact that it was not in America, and the standards of quality might be elevated. I was sadly mistaken. The food had the same greasy American taste, and that was the last time I was going to gamble on foreign fast food. As I walked back to the car, I continued to be in awe of how it felt like I was in some part of the US. For the most part, the clothing and cars were exactly what you would find back in the States. I made it a goal to stay away from the malls, because that's not what I went to Kenya for. I was in search of authentic Kenyan cuisine, and any local street shops full of arts and crafts.

Driving back to the bed & breakfast, the area looked like something you might find in a big southern city. Sure, much of the area appeared to be woods, but there were houses scattered throughout the trees. There did not appear to be a strong transportation system, so I saw a lot of people walking alongside the roads to get to their destination. Once we got away from the commercial areas, the residential sections seemed to be tranquil. My curiosity caused me to observe everything while driving through the countryside, but usually when I'm in transit, I am distracted by my phone. However, when I am in a foreign country, I enjoy just looking out the window and attempting to figure out what's going on in the city. It's a personal improvement that I'm proud of, because at my last place of employment, I would wake up, drive to work and back, and ignore everything that I drove past. Traveling has truly helped me to slow down and observe my surroundings, while also noticing the people in the area.

My plan to take a bus out of Nairobi and go to Tanzania started falling apart when I couldn't find a reliable company that would allow me to hike Mt. Kilimanjaro along the way. When I say "hike," I only mean that I wanted a couple of hours to walk up the mountain for a few hundred yards or so. The hike would be solely for the pictures and the experience because I am not that serious of an adventurer. I started to explore other options that could get me to Tanzania and allow me to see countryside along the way. I still had another day at the bed & breakfast, so I figured that I would walk around the neighborhood and see what type of community I was staying in.

I found my location on Google maps and looked to see if there was anything around me that was worth walking to. The map revealed some sort of community market at the end of the street. When I strolled down the rural block, I was able to see beyond the security gates on some properties, and it turned out that this neighborhood contained some high quality houses. No matter where I go, if I get the vibe that the community is safe enough to walk, I'll always tour the streets to get an authentic feel for the neighborhood. The security guards did not really appreciate me looking too hard at the properties, but I guess they could tell I was not from around there after their first glance. Once I reached the corner, I saw a commercial building that looked like it could be a mall of some sort, but did not appear to be open. I did notice a neighborhood street market that people were walking to and from, so I decided I would walk over and window shop, at the least. On the way, I saw a couple of barber shops, which were really only makeshift dividers sitting on top of an open grass lot. They did not look like the sophisticated barber shops that I would find back in Philly, but they did make me feel somewhat at home.

I had only been in Africa for a few days, so I was surprised that the locals did not look at me strangely or try to figure me out as I was walking around. I did actually try to fit in and act like it was a regular day and I was just simply walking to the store. A few years before my solo trip, I went to Paris with my two childhood friends, Marc and Alonzo, and the locals looked at us like we were from Mars. I still do not think we were dressed that much differently than everybody else, but one man even followed us around to find out what celebrity group we were. We could have worn pink rabbit suits and still possibly received less strange looks than when we wore our normal clothes. So after that encounter in Paris, I decided that I would try not to draw as much attention to myself on foreign soil.

As I walked closer to the local market, I started to notice that these weren't the usual shops where there's a variety of options like groceries or regional clothing. I started to get the vibe that this was not the type of market I was looking for, and since I did not know where I was, I decided I needed to return back to my room. My cardinal rule for solo travel is, if something does not feel right, you need to get back to where somebody knows you. There may not have been any danger waiting there for me, but I was not interested in finding out. I mainly came to Kenya to see a safari that they might not have in other places in Africa. If I wanted to hang among the locals in Kenya, my sister had close friends that could take me around to do so.

After my Mt. Kilimanjaro bus plans completely fell through, I decided that I would just catch a plane to Dar Es Salaam, Tanzania.

The best price for flights was for the next day, and I needed to book my hotel plans accordingly. I was disappointed that I did not get to see all of Nairobi, but Africa—and more specifically, Kenya—cannot be traveled in a day. This gives me a reason to come back. Since I did want to dine in style on my last night, I looked up the top restaurants on Yelp and found a Brazilian Steak restaurant that resembled Fogo De Chao in America. The location was not too far from where I was staying, and I was glad that I would not have a long trip. My sister, Joy, reminded me before my journey that Nairobi has Uber, a car service, which kept me from having to wait a while for the B&B's designated driver to arrive. When the Uber driver arrived, he locked in my destination and literally drove around the corner, and we were there in only about a minute. I would have walked, but it was dark and the location on Google Maps was not very clear. If I had known it was that close, I would not have wasted time and money to just put on my seatbelt and take it off in a matter of seconds. It was strange that they even had guards and a gate for the small strip mall where the restaurant was located. There was not much resistance to get in, but the guards were very thorough with checking who they allowed inside.

The only thing that might appear to be more strange than foreign solo travel is foreign solo dining. Everybody was in the steakhouse on a date, business meeting, or just out with the family. I, however, came for the food and the hopes of trying something different. I achieved that goal, but shied away when I was offered crocodile meat. However, I did take a liking to the cinnamon covered pineapple that was well-roasted. It was an amazing experience to dine with the locals, because sometimes when I go to nice restaurants in the States, certain people look at me like I do not belong there. As a foreigner, it just looked like the restaurant was a big family gathering, and each table just happened to be having their own conversation. I was satisfied with my night and trip and decided I would walk back to the room to get some sleep before my morning flight.

CHAPTER 6

The Island of Zanzibar

The process of leaving Nairobi turned out to be far easier than my arrival. Most airports in Africa are much less difficult to walk through than ones in America, where you have to walk past 50 New York City-like blocks just to reach your gate. The security was solid, but the terminal that I was leaving from resembled a setting that you might find at a private airport. The flight time from Nairobi, Kenya, to Dar Es Salaam, Tanzania, was only about an hour. I suppose that the in-continent security standards are slightly relaxed compared to flights headed to other continents. There was not a reliable screen to check for updates on any flights, so I felt like I was forced into the role of the customer who was paranoid about missing his plane. Fortunately, I was not the only person feeling that way, because there were people who were booked for different destinations who had that same alert and confused look on their face.

After I continuously bothered the gate agent about departure times, my flight was finally called to board and ready to leave for Tanzania. The flight was very short and inexpensive. However, I had to earn my discount by listening to a five-minute long recitation of their customer loyalty programs as we landed. When I got off the plane, I prepared myself for another foreign tax debate, after my eventful customs trip in Kenya. After the usual jockeying for position with other passengers to be first in line to get cleared by customs, we were immediately stopped by what looked to be a doctor. There was a man in a white coat stopping everybody, looking for the yellow vaccination form that recorded all of our shots. I was sure to keep that in my wallet, and the officials really made it seem like that form was more important than my passport. Up until that point, I was under the impression that you needed the vaccination shots just so you would not get sick, and they weren't actually mandatory to enter countries.

Cruising past the first medical checkpoint, it was now time to pay for the country's visa "cover-charge." I cannot remember how much I paid, but I was not looking to pay the fare, whatever it was. I joked with the official that my ancestors were originally from Africa, and I shouldn't have to pay for the visa, because I'm "ancient family." He smiled and responded, "They shouldn't have left." I began to realize that the funniest encounters are usually with the custom agents and officials at African airports. Luckily, on this trip, I did not have to worry about any surprise tariffs or charges, and it was a rather smooth entrance to Tanzania. I flew into the city of Dar Es Salaam to get a glance of the mainland city before going to the island of Zanzibar. I knew I would have to catch a cab in order to reach the ferry, but I just was not sure how difficult the process would be.

Exiting the airport, I was met by a small crowd of taxi drivers, just like in Kenya. This time the faces were more pleasant, because it was now the afternoon and not 4AM like it had been when I arrived in Nairobi. I told an older taxi cab driver that I was going to the ferry for Zanzibar, and he said he would take me over there and give me proper directions to avoid the all the salesmen. I took his initial fare suggestion at face value because I did not feel like negotiating and because he had an honest demeanor about him. It had crossed my mind to spend a night in Dar Es Salaam, but my plan was to start in Zanzibar and work my way back to the mainland if I wanted to. At this point, I was not really sure what country was next after Tanzania, and there was no time constraint, so I did not feel pressured about which path to take.

The drive to the ferry was interesting, because all I can remember is a long road from the airport to the dock. For the majority of the road, the sides were lined with people either tending to their market stalls or just hanging out. It reminded me of back home in Philly on 52nd Street, where vendors have their tables set up and attempt to sell you on whatever goods they're offering. Here I was, thousands of miles away from home, and I was starting to feel comfortable, because I could identify with the atmosphere. Two different areas of the world that probably know nothing about each other seemed basically identical to me. I was back to my spectator role in the passenger seat once I witnessed the everyday hustle of Dar Es Salaam.

Traffic was not actually cruising, so I had a lot of time to observe each area thoroughly. I noticed that there were two unusual aspects to the traffic on the road. In the States, you might have an occasional person in between the streets trying to sell you something when you are sitting at a red light, but Africa is far more business driven. When our car was stopped on this road in Dar Es Salaam, at least four or five people would bring their stores to us. They were selling everything from freshly roasted peanuts to water bottles, clothing, or jewelry of some sort. Some were quick to move on if we did not respond, and others would hold it in front of us to see if we'd budge. Throughout this whole ride, not one person simply asked me for money—I only encountered people selling their goods. Another part of the traffic was the young guys riding on their motorbikes, weaving in and out of the cars. In a way, it was like the guys riding their dirt bikes in Philly, but these bikes in Tanzania were road-certified and seemed to be very popular.

During the ride, the cab driver was kind enough to briefly explain the city and country, as well as what I could expect. He also was determined to give me thorough directions on how I was to conduct myself once he dropped me off at the ferry. He described the most cost-efficient and cleanest ferry that I could take, and the amount that I should pay. He said that when I got out of the car, I needed to carry my own bags and avoid the tons of guys out there asking if they could help me or trying to get me to their ferry. He told me not to look anybody in the face and not to say anything as I walked onto the ferry. At first, I thought he was just trying to secure a sale for his friends at a specific ferry, but his tone did not necessarily sound like a salesman's—he sounded serious. Now that I was somewhat experienced at passing through African checkpoints, I figured that he could actually be telling the truth.

Sure enough, as we arrived, there was a small crowd gathered just to get tourists and travelers to take their ferry. It was like someone had called ahead and said there was an American coming to the dock and that he had money to give away. I did just as the cab driver told me and did not say anything as I walked into the small building to pay the cashier. For me, it's never annoying when there are so many people trying to get me to use their services. In some ways it's a bit of a culture shock, because in the US, unless you are a known millionaire, nobody is pleading with an everyday Black man to get in his cab. So I took the heckling in stride and saw it as a positive that they actually wanted me to use their business.

There was about a 45-minute wait until the ferry left, so all the passengers were gathered at a waiting area next to the dock. I was expecting a small ferry that carried about 40-50 people, but when I saw the large crowd of people, I knew it couldn't be a small boat. As I sat down, a gentleman, who looked to be in his sixties and who spoke great English, told me about the different businesses that he had in Zanzibar. He was rather calm and did not have a salesman's tone, but he was quite confident in the jet skis and other entertainment services that he could offer. I really did not care for any sports entertainment while I was in Zanzibar because I was not traveling with friends. I was really only there to get to know the culture and relax on the beach. I politely declined, but I did notice that the strategy in his sales pitch was interesting, and I found it to be more effective than the usual cajoling.

There was a first class on the ferry, but the boarding process was basically every man for himself. I was surprised that the ferry was brand new and had a high class feel. I did not manage to get a window seat, but I was just happy to be comfortable, and I enjoyed the air conditioned interior. I had no intentions of straining to see the view outside, because I was content with relishing the fact that I was about to see a new culture in Africa. My main reason for going to Zanzibar was because I heard Malcolm X mention the island in an article or interview somewhere. I do not even believe he was actually able to see Zanzibar island outside of the airport, due to the visa situations being a little different in Tanzania at that period of time. But yes, Malcolm X's journey was a strong motivation for a lot of my travels and exploration.

Once I arrived in Zanzibar, I was surprised that there was another security check and that they wanted to inspect my bags. After rummaging through my well-folded clothes, the agent stained my bags with white chalk, and it was now time to find my way to my hotel. The trend became clear: regardless of the location of transportation in Africa, there's most likely going to be a crowd of official and unofficial taxi drivers waiting to offer you a ride. I'm not sure why, but I came up with the idea that the elderly taxi drivers were the most trustworthy and probably my best chance at getting a fair deal. I guess that can be classified as "ageism," but that's the honest vibe I got from all of my taxi trips.

If you do not have insider information or have never been charged the going rate in that area, then the chance is that you might pay too much for a taxi. One might say, "Just have a number in mind and try to stick close to it when bartering." That's tricky, because tourists usually have high numbers, and you also might not have a good idea on how long your trip will be.

In this instance, my hesitation to choose a cab driver caused one of the most bizarre scenes I've ever witnessed. Two taxi drivers were lobbying aggressively to get me to choose their taxi, and the closer I got, the louder they became. I really did not care who drove me to the hotel, I just wanted to get there safely. Of course, I chose the older gentleman and figured the yelling would die down as it usually does. The other taxi driver felt that the older driver stole me from him, so the yelling in Swahili continued. I thought it would be a quick spat, but it dragged on for at least a minute before I was able to leave. I realized from then on that I had to figure out a solid system for picking out cab drivers and stick to it because being unsure causes confusion. This encounter gave me more ammunition when it came to trying to convince Black people to travel to Africa more. This is a place where even the taxis fight over serving you, so how can you turn that down?

The driving experience through Zanzibar was mostly the same as in Dar es Salaam, as people were hanging out on the street with the various sidewalk markets. At this point in my life, I hadn't really been to any of the islands in the Caribbean, so I was not familiar with the island lifestyle. Indeed, this was my first time in Zanzibar, but it felt like each neighborhood had some sort of family feel. This was another chance to stare out the window and admire Africa during my ride, and I focused on attaching myself to different individuals' missions. Some people were transporting their goods through the streets, balancing bags on top of their heads, and others were keeping their small markets in order while waiting for the next sale. Each cab ride was turning into a small movie with the greatest script, just watching people live their lives.

Based on the reviews, the hotel I chose was voted the second best in that region of the island. The best hotel in the area was priced around 300 dollars a night—clearly a place for men trying to impress their wives on their honeymoon. The hotel where I was staying was called the Tempo Hotel, an old building that they were currently renovating. The building was very colorful, with stained-glass and an open structure that let the sun and fresh air flow through. It was a very old-school building with skeleton keys, so I predicted that this was going to be an interesting stay.

My room was a nicely sized space that featured a wooden Swahili four-poster bed. It was clear that mosquitoes were a real problem, because the bed had a net around it so guests could sleep in peace. The bathroom was nicely crafted with a Moroccan tile designed tub that also served as the shower. The design and color were great, but I'm not too big on Moroccan tiled showers because they're not easy to clean thoroughly. The room overlooked the pool and had a small deck once you opened the doors. I'm 6'5" and have broad shoulders, so squeezing onto small balconies to eat my meal did not interest me much. I also couldn't see myself spending much time in my room since it did not receive much sunlight and the bed looked to be the only comfortable furniture that I could relax on.

Luckily, my room was next to a lounge area that had a pool table and nice couches to relax on while the air was flowing through the open windows and doors. The lounge also had a patio that had a great view of the beach and the rest of the area. The hotel was an old building, but the designers had done a great job of letting the actual island be the highlight. The weather is usually perfect on Zanzibar, so there was no real reason to try and outdo what was already there. The hotel design allowed the building to be immersed in the climate. After one glimpse of the setup outside, I could already envision eating my meals there while looking at the water. Another great attribute of Zanzibar is that there was not a "cheap and cheesy resort" atmosphere, and everything about the people and service felt genuine.

My first day was winding down, and I decided to get a freshly prepared dinner at my hotel. Once I sat at the table and devoured my dinner while watching the sunset, I knew that Zanzibar was a place that I'd be visiting for the rest of my life. You can buy that setting on almost any beach, but in Zanzibar it feels natural and relaxed. I had the outdoor restaurant and hotel pool behind me, locals playing on the beach in front of me, and the sun was clear in the sky. I honestly began to question why this island was not swamped with tourists or even people from Dar Es Salaam. I didn't complain, because the setting was peaceful and a great end to a day of travel.

If there was one thing that was annoying, it was the flies. They buzzed around my food while I was trying to eat. Back in grade school, my friends and I would always question why some people in the African documentaries never swatted the flies away. Now I knew for sure that trying to swat the flies in Africa all day would be pointless. The first day, the flies may have bothered me a bit, but I slowly stopped caring and just let the flies pester me. I bonded with the servers at the hotel and they were glad to hear that I was from America and had come to visit them. Based on the way instructions were being handed down, it appeared that the hotel was owned by Arabs, and the natives of the country filled most of the labor-intensive jobs. Despite this being a small observation, it let me know that I needed to pay closer attention to who owned what industries and properties in Africa.

I was looking forward to enjoying my food in peace, like I would in any country, but the Zanzibar street salesmen were very aggressive, and they had no problem walking by to show me the clothes they were selling. I heard that common greeting, "my brother," and when I looked up, there would be a guy smiling with his arms open. At first, I did the usual American "I'm not interested" nod while I went back to eating my food. Then, he mentioned a rather cheap price for a couple of dashikis that looked pretty nice. I did not have any cash, but I told him to come back and find me, even though I was sure he would, anyway.

When the sun started setting, it was the perfect chance to take one of those postcard picture walks on the beach after my meal. This beach was rather small, with only about three or four hotels obtaining a space in front of the water. I was staying next to a prestigious and expensive hotel, and they had a high class private pool that was almost sitting on top of the beach. In my book, if you pay 300 dollars, you deserve all the fixings and a little more on top. I'm not sure if I've seen a better view than an orange sky while walking on soft sand in beautiful weather. I had only been in Zanzibar for a day, but I was already planning on telling all my friends about this serene place on the far side of Africa.

The night went pretty smoothly, even though it was my first time sleeping with a mosquito net. I'm not sure how it happened, but some flies managed to get inside the netting. I swiftly eliminated those threats to my comfort.

I awoke to a high quality breakfast. The hotel had a great mixture of local cuisine mixed with American breakfast downstairs in the open dining hall. The breakfast was a great head start, because I had a big day of exploration and I knew that I might be on the road for a bit. I had done a great amount of research on Zanzibar and its different landmarks, so I wanted to check those off the list on the first full day. I was amazed to find out that Freddie Mercury from the rock group Queen had lived in Zanzibar during his childhood. Even though Freddie passed away in 1991, he still had a house on the island that tourists are allowed to visit. I walked up the stairs and saw a few pictures of Freddie on the wall, but nobody was at the desk to receive me. After no one answered, I accepted my small victory of at least visiting the building and seeing a couple of pictures.

My second trip of the day was to Nungwi Beach, on the north side of the island. There was no official transportation system, so I had to find a reasonable driver to get me there. A few older taxi drivers always hung out next to the hotel, so I was sure that the hotel staff were familiar with them. One gentleman, Anwar, gave me a rate that I estimated to be reasonable, and I decided to use his services. Nungwi Beach was on my radar because of all the reviews that said that this specific beach had clear water. I rarely swim in water that I cannot see through—the thought of a jellyfish or shark sneaking up on me is one I'm not comfortable with. I also wanted to see a different part of the island, since I know most areas have their own identity, and I would be limiting my adventure by staying in one neighborhood the entire visit.

Anwar spoke pretty good English and explained that the trip would be about an hour and a half. I saw this as another opportunity to sightsee on the way as we went through the different neighborhoods. Initially, it was more of the same, with small markets and people hanging around in the street while the sun beamed down. The driver showed me the areas that were going to be improved upon in the near future. He explained that the area we were driving through, which was not too far from my hotel, was going to have more hotels built along the water. Even though many people still do not know that Zanzibar is a treasure, somebody does, and is looking to expand.

As we got farther away from the hotel, the scene transitioned to a rural setting, and the houses became more spaced out. There was no sign of asphalt now, as the roads were all dirt and there weren't any sidewalks for pedestrians to walk on. Even though this was a well-traveled road, not much time had been put in to make it very drivable. As we continued down the road, I realized that we were just driving through small towns and neighborhoods the entire time. We did not run into any other vehicles on the road very often, and when we did, we both had to drive a little on the shoulder to get by. Nothing felt strange about the travel experience, but it was indeed much different from the rural roads I was used to. There appears to be much land and space throughout the island, but the road to Nungwi beach was consistently narrow.

It's been reported that Zanzibar is almost entirely Muslim, and it showed once I saw the school uniforms of the children. The road runs through a strip of schools and all the young ladies had identical khimars on as they made their way home at the end of the school day. Khimars, also known as hijabs, are a covering worn by Muslim women on top of their heads. Even though the climate is rather hot in Zanzibar, the kids had on formal clothing and the uniform appeared to be strictly enforced. Along the way, I saw a few mosques, where men left their shoes outside so they could go in and pray. These mosques were far from the gigantic mosques I've seen around the world—they were more like brick ranch homes that had become acknowledged places of prayer. The island is listed as about being 99% Muslim, but I did not get the idea that they throw their religion in your face. It appears to be the way of life for the island, but I never felt like an outsider because my beliefs are different.

I was surprised that this part of Zanzibar still had cows doing agricultural work, having been heavily trained by America to always expect new technology. I'm not referring to the plump, steroid-filled cows that you might find in the US, but these were skinny and walked extremely slow. Every cow appeared to be a worker.

While some worked in the field, others were used to transport goods on the road. The roads had houses directly to the side of them, but it looked like they had open fields behind them. I'm not sure if most of these people were farmers with crops, or if it was simply open land that was unused. My visual calculations could be off, but there appeared to be an abundance of land space in these rural areas.

I expected a top-of-the-line, resort-like venue when I arrived at Nungwi Beach, but it was the complete opposite. The road was uneven, with a bad foundation, and there was no great welcoming sign. We had to drive through a neighborhood of small shops that looked like they could be makeshift houses. There was nothing wrong with their setup, in my opinion, but I was surprised that this site was not developed. There weren't many people at the beach, and I was not sure if it was because it was not a heavy travel season or if it was just an exclusive area. The aesthetics really did not matter to me at all, I just wanted to see the blue water. There appeared to be a couple of hotels by the water, but nothing too luxurious. They simply added to a setting that matched a small beach town look.

The Tanzanian taxi drivers usually have no problem going on a day trip with you, because there isn't a guarantee that they'll get another customer if they stay where they are. It may make sense to negotiate a round trip rate, because you can secure a ride, and the driver can secure a sale. The driver was kind enough to watch my things while I went swimming, which meant I had one less thing to worry about while I watched out for jellyfish and sharks. When I got up to the water, it was clear, and the ocean floor was easily visible. That comforting sight gave me the courage to swim without a worry of any water predators. Even when I was about fifty yards into the water, I could still see how light blue the water was and I was immediately satisfied with my choice. This was the perfect beach atmosphere because there were only about six people on the small beach, and it was a rather peaceful day.

It was an extremely hot day, and the water was fairly warm, and there were only a few clouds in the sky. I was never much of a swimmer, since I rarely went to the beach back in the US, and I tend to stay away from the pools inside gyms and recreation centers. I found this to be the perfect time to practice my swimming strokes while I had the space and clear water. Almost instantly, I found my rhythm for treading water and swimming long distances. Something as simple as space and peace was the only thing I needed to feel comfortable swimming in deep water. The only drawback is that I did not realize that this body of water is basically liquid salt, and if you go under water, it will feel like your eyes are bleeding. My swimming practice came to an abrupt end as I raced back to shore to save my eyesight. I only returned to do some leg exercises in the shallow water before I was done swimming.

I could only see a few restaurants around, and I went with my driver's recommendation. The restaurant he suggested sat right on the sand, and the menu selections were all derived from African cuisine. The food was great, but it was nowhere close to being the highlight of the meal. I only ordered a glass of orange juice before the meal, but it took a long while for the beverage to be served. Once the waitress brought the orange juice out, I took a sip, and then realized why it took so long to make. It was fresh orange juice that had been made on the spot, and it tasted better than any orange juice I had ever had. Right there, I realized that whatever orange juice they serve us in the States, it has to be of lower standard than the pure orange juice that I was served at this restaurant. I would have ordered another orange juice, but I felt bad that that the waitress/bartender would have to do all that work for one glass at such a low price.

An unexpected mix of pleasure and learning new things made Nungwi Beach another successful adventure. The ride home was yet another chance to get an understanding of the island and its inhabitants. My driver explained to me that most of the country is poor, and government officials and the people who own the hotels are usually the only people who are well off. The citizens are hard workers and do a lot to make ends meet, but it is obviously far from easy. Many of the houses have a nice outer shell made of rocks that can be found around the island. From what I saw, the quality of house structures stops there. There weren't many proper windows, and some of the places were literally just a shell of a house. I was not sure, but there may not have to be much more to the houses, because Zanzibar has a rather hot climate. As we drove back through the towns, I saw some butcheries, but not many stores on the road. I figure that many families and neighborhoods do the work themselves when it comes to providing food. There weren't any McDonald's or fast food places present, and convenience stores were almost non-existent, so people cannot get a quick meal.

I finally had an understanding of why some business settings were so competitive, and why the people had to be aggressive with their sales pitches. Opportunities and money do not present themselves often for the locals, so the quickest sale might be to a tourist. When I arrived back at the hotel, I ran into street sellers I had met earlier in the day, and I was happy to purchase whatever clothing or craft pieces they had. One seller even bragged to his friends that he had made a sale, holding up the money. Another man explained to me that that he had yellow fever and really had no means to eat at all, so I was more than willing to buy a few things from him. One thing I learned about Africa is, no matter what someone's situation may be, not one person asked me for money outright. All the guys wanted was for me to buy what clothing, crafts, or food that they had for sale, so they could handle their various affairs.

I'm always careful about acknowledging that I'm fortunate to be born in a place where resources are readily available. I'm not really sure how and why this situation is possible in the US and not in other places. I was, however, able to see another situation where healthcare may not even be a valid option, and starting a business would be extremely difficult. It did not appear that the street selling was completely about the money, but more about someone using their services and being able to sell something. I believe that it would be beneficial for more Americans to start traveling to Zanzibar, because the supply and demand would be satisfied equally. More specifically, I honestly believe that the locals felt comfortable with me and were happy that I was there. The small amount of money that we take for granted and carelessly spend on things we do not need could help the inhabitants of Zanzibar a great deal, and, even better, boost their morale.

I spent the next day relaxing and walking around the island, as there never seemed to be a reason for me to fear for my safety. The day did not lack drama, though, as I witnessed a child drowning while I was at the beach. A big crowd gathered while a few tourists ran to try and revive the young child. I tried not to lose hope, but the fact that I did not see any lifeguards or medical assistance was disturbing. I was thankful to God that the tourists were able to revive the child and the ambulance came later to take him to the hospital. It was amazing that everyone worked together to save this child, and we were all relieved that the day was able to go on without tragedy.

After a day or so, my body got used to the climate of Zanzibar, and I started to have ideas about where I might be living later in my life. I only wore flip-flops after my first day on the island because it felt too hot for shoes. I have very sensitive skin, but lotion, cocoa butter, and petroleum jelly were pointless in Zanzibar. I was shocked that my skin was hydrated 24/7 without having to apply anything. It was the same case for my hair, which is always dry and usually needs some form of oil or grease, but my hair couldn't have been more hydrated and shiny if I had used a whole bottle of Soul Glo. This has never happened to me in Miami, Los

Angeles, Spain, or any other hot climates. I took this as a message from God that this is where I'm really from.

I decided to cap off my trip with a visit to the most luxurious hotel on the island and see what they had on the restaurant menu. When I walked through the giant wooden doors, I realized why they charged so much for one night's stay. The extravagant look and heavenly ambience was something that I'm sure most high rollers would expect when they stay at a hotel. Everything was well polished, clean, and bright to the point that you would have thought you were in Paradise. The service was so phenomenal that I almost felt like I was a billionaire. The restaurant had a great view of the beach, and I could still see the water with the moon's reflection flowing with the waves. I had lamb soup and a Moroccan-style lamb and rice dish as I appreciated my view of the water. The dinner service was first-rate, and I walked out of that hotel feeling incredibly fortunate to have experienced it.

From the first time I rode through the streets of Tanzania, it felt like home, and that feeling never changed. In my eyes, Zanzibar is a no-brainer for a vacation, and more people should travel there. Not only was I able to do the conventional vacation activities, but I also learned more about a different culture and witnessed their strong work ethic. As soon as I arrived, I knew that this would be a place I would consistently travel to.

CHAPTER 7

Parisian Nights

It was fun to bounce from country to country in Africa, but I was exhausted from the constant flying and lack of stability. I initially wanted to go from Tanzania to Ethiopia or Morocco, but I decided I would go to a city where I knew I could stay for an entire month. A year before my long trip, I had stayed in Paris for a month to see if I could live outside the US for more than a couple of weeks. That month proved to be one of the most enlightening months of my life, letting me learn about myself and other cultures. I concluded that if I went to Paris now, I could work on my French and also search for basketball teams in the surrounding areas. Paris also had several high quality basketball gyms and fitness centers that I could use to stay in shape. My previous month in Paris was during a frigid October, so I was looking forward to enjoying the month of May leading into the summer.

France is a country that I love to travel to because there are a great number of Africans present, so I never feel out of place. When I traveled from Africa to Paris, I still experienced a big culture shock, because the climate felt terribly mild and I went from seeing all people of color, to occasionally seeing a few. The rules and economic systems in France are completely different, as well. Africa is great for tourists who want to negotiate for bargains, while Paris basically forces tourists to pay top dollar for everything. Instead of a group of taxi drivers waiting for me, I had to pay ten Euros or so to board the Réseau Express Régional (RER) train from Charles De Gaulle Airport to get inside the Paris city limits. I couldn't wait to finally settle in, because I was far too tired to keep dragging all of my bags around from country to country.

The first time I spent a month in Paris, I stayed in Montparnasse, a neighborhood in the southern part of the city. Since I'm coming from Philadelphia, I honestly think I'm comfortable staying in almost any neighborhood in Paris. So I considered choosing what borough to stay in to be of small importance. In the case of Montparnasse, I saw it as upscale and highly convenient, featuring an outdoor market with all the vegetables and cuts of meat that you could think of. There's also a main metro station in the area and plenty of restaurants and shops along the main avenue. I would start my days in Montparnasse and venture off into the city with the intent of getting a better understanding of the "City of Lights." The walk from Montparnasse to the Eiffel Tower or the Louvre was always interesting and encouraged me to stop taking the train altogether after the first week.

On this trip, I decided to choose a Parisian neighborhood that was around the basketball gym that I was going to join. The suburb of Aubervilliers was the site of my desired gym, so I searched anything that was in North Paris or the surrounding suburbs. I found a nice place on Airbnb next to the Porte de Pantin metro station, which did not appear to be a long walk to the gym. My preference was to rent an apartment that only I would be staying in, because at the time, the thought of staying with strangers for a month seemed weird. I had never stayed in a studio before, but I was not bothered, because I did not plan to spend much time in the apartment anyway. A lot of space in a house is something I enjoy, but never seem to use efficiently, for whatever reason. In the two houses that I've purchased and lived in myself, I've really only used my bedroom, kitchen, and another room for a music studio. I did not really see it as a problem if all three were condensed into one space—especially in Paris.

Antoine, the apartment owner, was kind enough to explain all the particulars of the neighborhood and anything else that I should look for. The apartment was small but had everything I needed, and I was just glad to be back in Paris for at least a month. However, a room on the fifth floor in a building without an elevator was going to be a challenge. I had to get in basketball playing shape anyway, so I was up for it. Antoine gave me a brief tour of the neighborhood and showed me which restaurants to stay away from, due to some health violations that had not yet been caught by the officials.

Overall, the neighborhood had a totally different personality than Montparnasse, but it still had the same clean and welcoming feel to it. There was a concert house across the avenue called La Villette, so I calculated that being around a landmark would mean that I was in a highly demanded area. By looking at the map, there was no hint that a walk from my apartment to the heavily touristed Notre Dame section would be as eventful as my last Parisian trip.

One drawback to my location was that there was a McDonald's directly down the street from me. I'm well aware that the business development schemes are far different than those in the States, but I was hoping for a convenient outdoor market like in Montparnasse. Whatever the case, I happened to see a few appealing restaurants as I passed through the streets, so that encouraged me to stay optimistic about the area I was staying in.

It was time to get back in shape, so my vacation was technically over. I woke up the next day, ready to explore this new trail to the basketball gym. Based on the directions on my phone, it appeared that all it would take was a walk around La Villette, and I would be there in twenty minutes or so. I hadn't realized that La Villette has a river with some parks and a science building behind it. It's very important to walk as much as you can when you are in Paris, because if you take taxis and trains, you may miss a lot of attractions that are only minutes away from your hotel or apartment. Throughout the entire walk through La Villette and the science building, there was a long, canopy-like covered walkway, which I figured was helpful on the rainy days. It was a bit different when I crossed into the suburbs, because I had to walk along what looked like a dirty green river to get to the gym. The sides of the river were painted with artful graffiti, but this did not look like the place to hang out when enjoying a beautiful day in Paris.

The gym was called the Hoops Factory, and it was state of the art, with new hardwood courts and a nice lounge on both floors. The only thing I really cared for was to have my own court to work out on and an extended amount of time to do so. The director on sight was a gentleman of African descent who introduced himself as Coach Black and spoke great English. My French at this point was still limited, and most natives could pick up on that easily. The Hoops Factory had a great system in place, where the morning and most of the afternoon is open for anyone who wants to work out individually or in a group. For an hour or two during the afternoon, the gym is only open to the youth, and they did a great job of organizing the programs during those times. I already had the idea of bringing the same vision to Philly, but being able to see this in the flesh made it realistic and more of a possibility for me.

One of my lifetime goals is to speak French fluently, so in essence, basketball was only one reason for coming to France. I knew that to bring my fluency to fruition, I would have to speak to a lot more with people, even if I did not care to. I'm not even great with small talk in *English*, so I knew this would be a difficult challenge for me, even if I was ready to take it on. Throughout my life, the basketball court has served as my golf course for networking, where I just happen to meet people and forge friendships from there on. It's never been intentional, but instead something that happens naturally. A friendship often may develop from the teamwork or the competition in a basketball game. As the days went on, I learned that you can gain friends in a different way while playing basketball in France.

When I came to Paris the prior year, the Hoops Factory hadn't been built yet, and I had been searching feverishly for any place where I could run a game of 5-on-5 basketball. I just happened to stumble on a gym where they had pickup basketball every Sunday night at 11. The greatest part was that the gym was not too far from my apartment in Montparnasse, so I could walk back and forth. There was a 3-on-3 system that they had going, and my two teammates invited me to a Sunday Crossfit workout the following week. This outdoors Crossfit group provided me with the chance to stay in shape and to meet some lively French people. I met a fellow American at the courts named Jason who helped me out when I did not understand everything being said in French. He told me that it took him a whole year to find a gym to play basketball, which showed me that you'll find things depending on how badly you want them. Jason told me that it took him about twelve years to consider himself fluent in French, and that he had help from his Francophone wife and her family. My ego took a slight hit when I learned this, as I wanted to be fluent in four years total.

I only went to the Hoops Factory to do drills, exercises, and work on my game by myself. I even went to restaurants by myself so I could enjoy the food. As the days went on, I began to understand that the concept of doing things alone was not too common, and actually seemed strange to some in Europe. Some Europeans see a restaurant as a great place for fellowship and sharing conversations. I've only seen restaurants as a great place to get a tasty meal and try something different. Even so, I figured that if I was in France long enough, the people might be able to change my thinking.

Some French people can actually pick up the vibe that you are not from France and also cannot speak the language. What's even more impressive is that they can sense that you are American—all without you having to say a word! I met most of my friends and workout buddies at the Hoops Factory because I either did not know how to answer in French or I did something that was completely out of the norm. Once my future friends found out that I was an American, they were extremely helpful and generous. They were all more than willing to help me improve my French and find places that I might need to go in the city. I instantly thought back to all the times I could have been in that position in the US and what the chances were that someone would have helped me how they did. When I thought about it, I had to take a deep look at myself, and I honestly do not think I would have done the same thing for a foreigner at the gym.

My first two friends were looking to do workouts together and introduced themselves as Keyvan and Ibrahim. Their names are pretty common, but it took me a while to understand the French way to pronounce them. French nouns are something that I'm going to struggle with for a lifetime, because they do not sound anything like they're written. I was appreciative of the offer to workout, since it allowed me to feel like I was a part of the city and they treated me like I had been their American cousin for years. This welcoming atmosphere and attitude is something that we have to work on in America, or at least the in the places that I have lived. It's rare for someone to invite a foreigner, who does not speak their language, to train with them, especially when they already have a workout partner.

My French was elementary, but they assured me that they weren't going to be dumbing down their speech just so I could feel like I was fluent. Even if I had been fluent in proper French, it may not have mattered because my ears could tell that French slang is a completely different language. At that stage of my French fluency, I really could understand what someone was saying, but the slang spoken by most millennials and those even younger was completely different. I was shocked until I equated it to someone who speaks perfect English maybe not being able to decipher the conversations between my friends and me back home. I sincerely felt that I was picking up the words in French pretty fast, so the slang was not too difficult of a task. After an extensive day of basketball workouts, I was able to practice my French while eating pastries on the way home with my new friends.

Even if it were possible, I'd be too embarrassed to go back and do the accounting on how much money I've spent on pastries in France. Cookies, donuts, and tarts are something I've never really cared about when in America. Even in Montparnasse, I initially shied away from the bakeries if I was not looking for a baguette. Once I decided to try a Pain au Pomme, I haven't been the same since. My description will not do it justice, but I'll try to explain what a Pain au Pomme is, because I feel it's necessary. Pain au Pomme basically means apple bread, and it's like a coffee roll, but the dough is more complex and the apple filling is like pie filling— but far better. The quality of the taste and presentation is something that I haven't seen matched anywhere. Of course, I had to return to my favorite patisseries when I finally made it back to Paris. A simple Pain au Pomme in the park became the highlight of my day more often than not during my first trip to Paris.

My new neighborhood of Pantin might've been challenging simply because of the red flags that the apartment owner pointed out to me. I saw a few things that validated his suspicions, but I will not share them because I'm taking an aggressive approach on keeping this book positive. The highlight of Pantin had to be the patisserie at the top of my street. For one Euro, you can purchase the best baguette in town (in my opinion) and then add whatever you'd like, ending up with a great meal. Sometimes the line would be out the door and down the street because the baguettes are so well-prepared. For lunch, they prepared sandwiches to your liking, and I was awed by how convenient it was to find a great meal in Paris.

I prefer to buy my baguettes from the bakeries outside the franchise markets, but the aroma of fresh bread is still present in the local chain stores. The supermarkets are a slightly different experience, and they may come as a bit of a culture shock for someone from the US. The first thing that may hit you is the awkward smells that French markets have. Various French cheeses have a strong smell, and the odor may hit you hard when you walk by the dairy aisle. The common markets also carry many of the poultry and cuts of meat that we might consider a delicacy in the States. Veal, duck, rabbit, and all cuts of lamb are typical products that are sold in the meat section.

It was a dream come true when I saw a butcher shop directly across the street from my apartment. And, two doors down, a reasonably priced fresh fruit and vegetable store. There were also two small markets down the street, which meant I did not have to leave my neighborhood if I wanted to prepare a meal. The people in the boucherie (butcher) were so pleasant every time I came to their store. It's a delight to walk into family owned stores in France, because they genuinely appear happy to see you. In America, it's possible to stop into a business whose employees greet you with a smile and a "hello," but I felt that welcoming atmosphere in almost every place in Paris. At times I would have to stop and wonder, "why is everyone so nice and always smiling?" Even more so outside of the tourist sections, the first worker you encounter is delighted to see you, and it's consistent in any butcher or bakery that I've been to in France.

I have to remind you that at this point in my Francophone journey, I couldn't completely understand French speakers, and my pronunciation of French words probably sounded like Spanish to them. One time I ordered Blanc de Poulet (chicken breast) in the boucherie and the clerk asked me to repeat myself five times. I even pointed to what I wanted, but somebody behind me had to give him the proper pronunciation so I could complete my order. That ordeal, and many others like it, caused me to be nervous whenever I went into stores. Sometimes if there were a few people behind me, I'd let them go in front me and act like I was still deciding because I was afraid I would keep butchering the language. I improved as time went on, and I learned to pick up how other people were ordering. I listened to the phrases they would use, and that turned out to be an effective method as the weeks went on.

During this trip to Paris, I began to truly feel like I was entering the exclusive club of expatriates that were getting to know the "real Paris." I decided to be a tourist one Sunday when the Louvre just happened to be free that night. The Louvre is currently the world's biggest museum, but it was originally used as a fort in the 12th century. The museum showcases a variety of art galleries that are based on many different cultures from several periods of time. It was clear to me that it would be impossible to see the entire museum in one night, so I made sure to learn what I could in the little time I had.

I'm comfortable admitting that I'm not great at being a tourist and the usual attractions do not interest me at all. When I took a trip to Los Angeles, I was more appreciative that I was able to play basketball in Compton and see the neighborhoods than to walk down the Hollywood Walk of Fame, which I was living down the street from. I love everything about Paris, but I had more of the same strange anti-tourist interests when I arrived there. I'm not sure how many months I've lived in France altogether, but I can say that I have never seen or attempted to see the famous "Mona Lisa". There are some things that do not resonate with me, and I think that every person should figure out what they want to see on a trip so they do not waste their time.

In terms of Paris, I got most of my inner tourist out the first time I went. I really made the effort to go to every museum there was that November. The museums were an important motivation for me, because they are something that I usually do not care to do when I'm in America. During that period, I had the pleasure of viewing a fascinating Andy Warhol exhibit. I also enjoyed the Hotel des Invalides and the intricate detail the museum designers used throughout the design of the building and the tombs. France is a place that takes pride in their history and their art, and they do an amazing job to make sure the public can access these places and works.

A lot of people fall into the tourist traps in Paris and miss out on the many things that I have listed because they're so eager to visit the well-known places. The Eiffel tower is an understandable desire, and, of course, the Louvre, but those two places can only tell you but so much about the wonderful city. I think the same goes for any tourist-heavy city that you travel to. If someone went on a vacation to New York City and only went to Times Square and the Statue of Liberty, you would probably feel as though they had missed out on the complete essence of the city. Along with the different neighborhoods of Paris, there are also different regions of the country of France that are well worth the trip. Many people feel obligated to only explore Paris, but there are so many great cities all over France, and they each have their own respective personalities.

For me, restaurants are just as important as museums, and in Paris, they are truly an experience. The quality gap for restaurants in the USA is so wide and inconsistent that I rarely go out to eat. In France, I've always found that you get a reasonable effort with any restaurant you stop in, and there's a higher standard for cooking. Paris is the main city in France, but there aren't many cheesy chain restaurants serving whatever they can get to the plate. In terms of influence, most of the fast food places in Paris probably came from the US. When I'm in Paris, I look online for any places close to my residence and use them as an opportunity to try something different.

Le Djembe was a restaurant that was on my street, but I had walked by it every day and not even known. The lunch and dinner schedules are slightly different in France than in America, so there may be times when you miss out on a restaurant or store because they're not open all day. I found out that Le Djembe is an Afro-Antillais (Caribbean) restaurant and their menu was appealing. The owners of the restaurant were happy to see an Afro-American stop by, and they greeted me with the little bit of French that I could understand. The lamb with rice that they served was exquisite, with creole flavors that were well thought out. The lamb appeared to be marinated in some sort of a mustard sauce, then grilled to perfection. The rice was accompanied with a red pepper and onion-based sauce that elevated the entire dish. They could tell that I had enjoyed the meal by how fast I finished it. The communication between us was limited, but we all understood that the appreciation was mutual.

One highlight of the neighborhood, which my apartment owner pointed out, was a steakhouse down the street called Au Boeuf Couronne. One late night, I was exceedingly hungry, but I hadn't made it to the grocery stores before they closed. I was surprised when, not only was the steakhouse open, but the place was rather busy. Au Boeuf Couronne is the type of restaurant where mostly everyone is in suits and formal attire. I did not get that memo, and I simply ate my meal in sweatpants. I was delighted to find that the staff did not treat me any differently despite my attire, and I never felt out of place eating amongst the French business class. The dinner service was great, and I believe everyone should experience that level of service at least once a year.

I had never seen the neighborhood of Pantin before I booked the room, but it turned out to be the perfect place for my accommodations. My days would flow so easily from start to finish during those spring and summer days. I would wake up and my trip to the gym would serve as a morning walk. After I finished working out, I would get any groceries that I needed for dinner and maybe buy a baguette and make a tuna sandwich. I usually spent lunch looking out my fifth floor window, eating my sandwich and observing the neighborhood. I'd go back to the gym to work out some more and come home after, to cook my dinner. There would be some sort of variation to those days if I decided I wanted to go sightseeing or hang with some friends.

Some days I would spend my dinner attempting to improve my French by watching televisions shows and movies. I rarely watch TV in America, but I knew that it was important if I wanted to improve my speech. It was difficult to comprehend French in person when I had first arrived in Paris, but it was far more challenging to understand what they were saying on the television shows. Day by day, I began to notice a slight improvement as I would stop and acknowledge when I understood a full conversation or recognize an uncommon word. French television is very different because the networks aren't as aggressive as America when it comes to advertisements. On some channels, they even cut out some commercials until the end. So if I was watching a program from the USA, when there was a spot where the show would usually go to commercial, the network would just transition to the next segment without one.

After my first month was over in Pantin, the owner told me that he would give me a deal if I wanted to occupy the studio for another month. I felt like it was a great deal, so I stayed another month so I could continue my regimen. The second month went fast, but this time the owner had a different tune about his current situation. It turns out that while I was staying at the apartment, he was staying in his girlfriend's apartment and those plans were starting to sour, so it was time for me to find something new. I knew it might be difficult to find another place that I liked for a reasonable price, but I thought it would be a great opportunity to find a new neighborhood.

I found a place in the northern suburb of St. Ouen and the pictures looked decent, so I thought that this would be a smooth transition. The neighborhood looked appealing when the taxi pulled up, but I was not sure why I couldn't find the apartment at first. Once I realized that the address number had been written in graffiti, I knew that this month was going to be interesting. The apartment owner was a nice young lady who led me into the apartment building, past the young guys hanging in the courtyard. In America, we might refer to these buildings and living situations as high-rise projects or low-quality apartments. This was a different country, however, and I wanted to wait before I drew assumptions. The flat was nice and had everything I needed, but the vibe I got from those young guys hanging outside was one of drug-dealing "corner-boys." It would not be so much of a problem if I was fluent in French and could understand what they were saying. If there was a problem, I needed to be able to hear if they were plotting and know what to say if there was a conflict. I decided I would stick it out, because I never felt threatened by any of the young guys after the first couple days. I had a couple of encounters where the guys may have mistaken me for a buyer, but after a while, they understood that I was a tenant.

My apartment in St. Ouen was only a five-minute walk from the city limits of Paris and the daily walk to the metro was always interesting, as I could notice the differences in quality of life in this section. The area still had nice soccer fields and parks, but there was an obvious prostitution hangout on the main avenue, and some of the streets weren't as clean as you might find in your typical Parisian neighborhood. On the weekend, vendors would gather in the street to collaborate for some sort of flea market, and the streets were always flooded with people looking for a bargain. This was not your conventional flea market, but more like everybody trying to sell the clutter in their house in the middle of the street. This neighborhood was different than the places I was used to in Paris, but it was nothing that I hadn't seen before in the States, so I was not too bothered by it.

One weekend came up and I noticed that Serena Williams was playing in the French Open tennis final. I'm not the type to look forward to watching sports events, mostly because I actually like playing in them so much. But I decided that I might be disappointed in the future if I looked back at having the chance see Serena Williams at the French Open but had simply stayed in bed because I was tired from workouts. I knew the final was about to start, but I was not sure if it would be postponed because of rain. When I arrived at the venue, I asked the security guard if I had the right entrance. He immediately blocked off the gate and asked if I had a ticket. I replied that I had no problem buying a ticket if they were still available, but I just wanted to know where I could get more information. The guard made it clear that this was an exclusive event and not one with a "silly atmosphere" that we might have in the States. His tone wasn't arrogant, but still managed to be amusingly condescending. I searched online and found that there were still tickets left to buy. I bought one and was able to gain entrance.

After walking up to the highest sections of the stadium, I exited the tunnel and was amazed at the large crowd. Using my admittedly humble French, I squeezed past the anxious spectators to get to my seat. Somehow, I instantly felt like the only person in the stands cheering for Serena. I also noticed that the crowd was clapping louder for the points of her opponent, Muguruza. This match was actually an opportunity for Serena to get into the record books for the most Grand Slam titles in women's tennis. She ended up losing, but I was still glad that I got the chance to see her play in person. Muguruza is from Spain, so it's possible that it was just European favoritism. I was unaware that Serena could speak French, but she addressed the crowd without speaking English at all. It's obviously easier to understand French when an American is speaking it, and I wish it was that easy with everyone else. When I watched this young woman from Compton speak French to a crowd at Roland Garros in Paris, it was just as inspirational as it sounds. I was so thankful that I had gotten out of bed to witness it. Fitness and basketball were a big part of my stay in Paris, and they were also how I got to meet a lot of people. The Sunday fitness class that I attended was strenuous, but it gave me a chance to connect with people my age from different cultures. They were even kind enough to invite me out to eat with them after the workout, which gave me a chance to get to know everyone better. Another one of my friends invited me to play in a basketball tournament in Creteil. It was great to see the diversity of the teams, and my team won the tournament. The longer I stayed in Paris, the easier I found it to meet new people and make more friends. Ironically, in 2015, when I first arrived in Paris, I was told that I would likely have a completely opposite experience. France is a part of Europe, but it holds a variety of cultures and stories, and that's why I enjoy being there.

CHAPTER 8

The South of France

After my stay in Paris, I came back to Philadelphia to be a counselor at a camp I had gone to as a kid. As I got older, I recognized this as an opportunity to push kids to imagine going places much farther than their own neighborhoods. By working with kids, I've learned that they're much more ambitious than adults, and easier to teach. Most adults might want to complete a task or a mission, but find excuses not to—or even worse, let fear deter them. When a kid has direction and help, he'll most likely work hard to achieve a goal if he has made up his mind to do so. My plan was to tell them of all the possibilities there are around the world, as soon as I got the chance.

My main goal after volunteering at camp was to find a basketball team to play for in Europe. I was sure that teams were going to want experience at some point, given that I was not directly out of college. I still hadn't been able to find a reliable sports agent, so I figured I would take a flight to France and meet the teams in person. I was hoping to at least workout with some teams in training camp and impress the coaches. I had already completed one workout with a team in Paris during my stay there, but they were not ranked high enough for me. Regardless, the team did not call me back, so it was safe to say it was not a great match.

During that workout, I met a couple of guys who told me that the teams in the south of France might be willing to pay more money, because most of the money around Paris was for soccer. As I spoke to other people in the French basketball community, I found that opinion to be consistent.

I decided my next flight would be to the south of France, but I did not exactly know where, because I was not too familiar with the cities. I knew of Monaco, but everybody talks about how expensive it is. I decided I would save that trip for when I was a little more financially confident. The most logical idea was to look up the basketball teams in the south and pick the one that made the most sense for me to visit. I decided to begin my trip wherever the cheapest flight was headed, and I would traverse from there. After a thorough search, it turned out that Nice, France, would be my next stop. This was an excellent location that provided multiple directions for me to go whenever I chose to leave.

At the time, I did not know much about Nice besides the fact that they had recently had terror attacks. Terror attacks in France truly disappoint me, because I think they paint a bad picture for a country that's not as violent as it would seem. France might be one of the safest places I've stayed, and it's a shame that its reputation gets ruined by a few tragic instances. I had just left Paris the day before the November 2015 terror attacks, and that gave me a perspective on the power of fear. The first month I spent in Paris was the safest I've had in my life, walking around alone at 1:00 in the morning after playing late-night basketball. It was a shock, after having this great month, to reach home and see the horror of what had happened. Family and friends are continuously worried about me when I travel, but I'm always quick to tell them that I feel the safest when I'm away from the US.

I knew that the atmosphere in Nice might be a little strange because the terror attack was still fresh, but I also knew that it was not what the city or the country was about. I decided to try another flight from Brooklyn because the prices were very low and I was confident in my ability to be on time. I took the Megabus and hopped on the train to JFK once I arrived in Manhattan, figuring that would be easier than a taxi. I made the mistake of getting off at the wrong stop, because I thought I had to switch trains, and that proved to be costly. Even so, I was still on time when I arrived at the gate, so I did not think there would be a problem.

I arrived at the check-in line with an hour and five minutes until flight departure, so I was glad when the gate employee allowed me to cut the line. I was immediately asked where I was going and the agents told me that they were going to make sure I got to the flight. Then, one employee signaled to another that there was a passenger headed to Nice, France. The agent radioed to another department and received the news that they would not take any more people or baggage because there was a VIP onboard. I was extremely disappointed, because I could understand if it was because I was late, but I was well within the rules, and they just wanted to make it a special flight for someone who was onboard.

I was told I had to call the airline's customer service so I could get a flight exchange for free. I called immediately and after holding for twenty minutes, I spoke with an agent who listened and said she would call me back in ten to fifteen minutes. After an hour with no call back, I called again and was placed on hold until the agent finally called me back after another hour and twenty minutes. She said there was nothing she could do, and I was own my own, denying she ever said she would give me the exchange for free. It was now almost three hours later and the system would not let me get an exchange flight. There were actually two flights that I could have boarded that night if she had acted quickly.

At this point, I really had no choice but to buy another flight and fill out a claim so I could get my money back later, as all of the flights had left for the night. I usually would tough it out, but I was not able to spend another night in the airport, so I left to stay in a hotel in Queens. The next day, I was so eager to get out of the country that I was about three hours early for my flight. It was going to be a different type of arrival, because my plane was landing at night and not in the morning like I had planned. After my Kenya trip, I realized that it is best to arrive at a city during the daytime if you have never been there before. I imagine that it's safer during the day, and it's also easier to see and assess your surroundings.

Even though it was dark, I was at least grateful that the weather was amazing in Nice when I arrived. I went looking for an information desk to see the best way of traveling to my hotel from the airport. It's a great idea to check online or find an honest source at the airport to learn about the cheapest way to get to your hotel other than a taxi. There may be a quick trip by bus or by train that may be near your hotel, especially if you are staying in a downtown area. Many people like to travel in style, but it's always better to save money that you can spend on your dinner that night. Most airports are far away from downtown, so a train might be the most efficient trip, as a taxi might get caught in traffic and take even longer.

I got back into my French mode and asked someone if there was a train that stopped near my hotel. There happened to actually be a bus that had a stop that was not too far from where I had to go. I had three bags with me, but I decided to go with the bus, because the weather was so great and I had no problem walking. I think everybody on my flight had the same idea, because the entire bus was packed and there was not much room to move. Luckily, the bus route was a straight shot to the beach area where I was staying and some people had already gotten off because their hotel was along the strip. I was well aware that I was in France, but I was amazed that I was getting a Miami vibe based on the bus ride alone. When I think of France, I usually think of its great city of Paris, but the warm climate of southern France was a completely different experience.

My hotel was a farther walk from the bus stop than I had expected and the room was small, but it was clean and plush on the inside. It did not have an amazing view or a single over-the-top luxury, but it did offer free water and ice cream, along with a free breakfast in the morning. I made sure to partake of these complimentary features. It had been a long flight, but I was anxious to walk the streets and see what Nice was like. I planned to walk around for a bit until I found a restaurant with the right menu for me. Whoever designed Nice was a genius with amazing style and vision. The weather by itself was impeccable, but the openness and colors accent the water and hills profoundly. As I walked through the city at night, it was like I was in the middle of a dream or a movie, and I was getting to see the beautiful sights up close.

I urge everyone to go to Nice and experience a summer night there. The tempo and the tone of the city is an indescribable combination that I have never seen before. Miami is comparable, but, of course, Nice has been standing for many more years, so the personality is a little more sophisticated. I became increasingly attracted to the city as I walked through the small, restaurant-lined streets as soothing music played all around. Many big European cities have the same attributes as their ancient towns and do a great job of enticing tourists, but still maintain the integrity of the city's history. Nice has perfected that balance, because although the scene was modern, it did not look like much had changed from years before. It was unfortunate that there had been a tragedy less than a month before, but the streets still looked alive and busy with tourists and natives.

I ended up walking around for an hour or so before I found a restaurant to my liking. I was heavily into Italian cuisine at the time, so an Italian restaurant was an easy and safe choice. The restaurant was settled in a small but busy street. It was amazing to have a front row seat to the constant entertainment of people walking past, while numerous street salesmen looked to catch their attention with flashing gadgets. I spoke of the crafts and goods that I saw from the street salesmen in Africa, but there is a slightly different supply in Europe. I suppose that the atmosphere is different because of the European laws. Most salesmen spend their time flying their gadgets in the air so that they flash in the night and get you to look up in amazement. Handmade crafts and clothes are what mostly catch my attention, but I guess the gadgets are intended to get the kids' attention and their parent's money.

Breakfast in the south of France is something that I have come to appreciate at hotels, because the selections are usually clean and tasteful. My hotel had a selection of croissants and baguettes to choose from, along with cereal, jams, and jellies. They also provided a generous variety of fruit to add an extra boost of energy to their guests' days. I was up rather early because I had slept a lot on the flight, and I was looking forward to getting a solid walk around the city before it became too hot. During the day, Nice is even better than at night because the colors of the buildings, water, and trees in the hills create a wonderful picture. I walked down to the boardwalk, and the scenery in the backdrop made my morning runs easy, no matter which direction I ran. The long main strip runs along hills that are covered with white houses and hotels. The view is a wonderful mixture of sky, coastline, and architecture. The memorial for the victims of the terror attack was still intact, so I stopped over to pay my respects. Actually seeing the site in person made it surreal that someone could turn such a beautiful place into a nightmare.

As a result of missing my flight, my stay in Nice got cut from three days to two, so it was time for me to focus on the real reason for taking the trip. My next stop was going to be in Avignon,

France, where I planned to meet with the basketball club SAP Vaucluse. My prayer was that Avignon would be similar to Nice, because that would make my decision to stay even easier. I took a direct train from Nice to Avignon and yet again continued carrying my heavy luggage through Europe. The ride was not too long, and I got to see the countryside of South France on the train. I decided to go with another Airbnb apartment that was not too far from the address of the basketball team. I envisioned going to see the city for a bit, then walking down to talk with the team in the hope of earning a spot.

My first impression of Avignon from the train station was that it was definitely an ancient town. The train station sits on a hill, and when you look down at the opening of the city, you see what looks like a cement fort. I had no real problem with the design, but I had a strong feeling that this place was going to be nothing like Nice. After doing some brief research on the city, I learned that Avignon and the surrounding towns had been under siege plenty of times throughout the centuries, so strategic architecture was necessary. As an American, I sometimes forget that buildings and structures could have been in place for more than 500 years.

My apartment was not far from the train station, and the walk through the streets reminded me of the Alamo in San Antonio. I did not see many examples of modern architecture, and even the restaurants had an old feel to them. The apartment where I was staying was without a doubt an ancient building, and the owner had not spent much time updating it. I mentally prepared myself to only focus on my basketball goals, so I put my tourist expectations to the side as I took a small tour of the city. When I walked through the busy sections of the city, Avignon appeared to be more of the same scenery, with stone streets and structures, but also an array of elegant shops and restaurants. Avignon was not the city of Nice at all, but it still had all the elegant attributes of a typical French town.

I located the team's address on my phone's map and headed out on what I thought was going to be a small journey. The directions took me outside of the city walls, which were still a bit interesting to see in the 21st century. The residential streets outside the city walls struck me as the ordinary type that you might find in a French town. The streets were clean, but did not necessarily have the glow that you might see in Paris. I was getting close to the address that was provided on the website, but for some reason I did not see a gym or team sign. The address led me to a basic house in a fairly nice neighborhood, but I knew that there had to be an error with either my map or the team's website.

There was an elderly lady in her yard, so I scraped together some courage and the best French words I knew and explained my situation. She told me that there was not a gym here, but there was a gym not too far from where we were, and she would have no problem taking me there. At this point, my French was not the greatest, so I had to confirm with her that she said that she was going to take me to the gym. It was unfathomable for me because I thought of all the years that I had lived in the US and how unlikely it seemed that somebody might do the same for me there. Here's a grown man (Black, if I may add), who can barely speak French, randomly coming up to a house, looking for a basketball court. I'm able to speak perfect English, and I'm from the US, but I still cannot imagine getting that type of generosity in my country. It just so happened that her grandsons had a workout that day at the same gym, so she said she could take me at the same time, but her willingness to help a stranger still amazed me.

During the short ride, the lady and her two grandsons were eager to hear about who I was and where I was from. It was an experience for me, but I guess even more so for them since a Black American man popped up at their gate. Throughout the conversation, I realized that my French was still rusty, and I might need to practice some more. One of her grandsons was able to figure out some of the words I mispronounced and also speak a little English himself. I was not blown away by the gym once we pulled up, but the interior looked to be well lit and well kept. This French woman was kind throughout our whole encounter and I thanked her excessively before I headed into the gym.

I saw that the first team was finishing up their practice, and the team looked solid, but I still saw myself being able to fit in. The coach came over and introduced himself to me, saying hello in French and then something that I did not understand after. I wanted to say, "Hi, I'm that shooting guard/small forward that you prayed for," but my French was not yet strong enough, so I settled for "bonjour." I spoke to the gentleman who takes care of the gym, and he told me that one of the team's presidents was in the back, and I could talk to him about a spot on the team. The facility was not as nice as the teams I visited in Paris, but the people seemed pleasant, and that counted for something.

My French was getting better the more I practiced, and I explained to the team director, Mr. Gautheret, how I could help the team. He explained that they had a limit on foreign players, but I could work out with the second team for a chance to work my way up. I was fully confident in my playing ability, so I was sure that it would speak for itself. The gym floor was so nice, with bright lights, that I couldn't wait to play and show them how great of a pickup I would be. I walked back to the apartment that night and got to see more of the town outside the city walls. There's a good mixture of races that make up the population, and I saw a lot of Arabian stores and restaurants along my walk.

My first apartment in Avignon was dated and on a small street, so I couldn't wait until the booking was finished so I could find another. The next apartment I found was outside the city walls and closer to the gym. The room was situated in a duplex with a small driveway and owned by a kind elderly lady who spoke slowly so I could understand her French. The apartment was very clean and had everything I needed, but there was no air conditioning, so it was a bit stuffy. The more I walked around Avignon, the more I began to like it. Avignon isn't extremely busy, and it's a place you can go and easily fit in. I also found a pizza place I liked that it was along the walk home from the gym, and that it had an easy-going owner. Mozzarella was not a main ingredient on most of the pizzas, so it was the first time I tried Emmental cheese. I spent a few nights devouring this new tasting pizza during my thirty minute walk home from practice. It was not bad, but it would not be my preference for cheese on a pizza.

The first basketball practice I attended was a bit difficult because I hadn't been in a real team practice in a while, and I was not exactly in mid-season form. For a team that was not on the highest level, they played pretty well, and I was able to get some good workouts in. Even though I came out of nowhere to be part of the team, the players were still open to help me out when I did not understand some French words. The team was incredibly receptive to me and some of the guys spoke to me after practice in a mix of French and English to get to know me.

I was really determined to show everybody that I was serious about playing on the team, and that my skills were at a high level. I gave 150% to every scrimmage, and played defense like it was the NBA Finals. I didn't miss many shots during our pickup games, and I dunked the ball if I got anywhere near the basket. I tried to look as much like Michael Jordan as possible, hoping that would force the team to give me a contract. After a few practices and exhibition games, I became comfortable with the system that they played, and I started to feel like I was apart of the team, even though I still had no contract.

I can admit that I sometimes get caught up in basketball and my creative projects and forget to live a little and spend time outside. I talked to my sister and told her I was in Avignon, and she immediately told me about grade school, when she sang about a bridge in Avignon. I'd never heard of the song or bridge, so I took the time to Google it and learn something. From the way I entered Avignon, I had never known there was a back section that had a bridge, and the pictures online were stunning. Immediately, I planned a day trip and was more than ready to explore another part of the city.

I walked through the city and saw that the rear section of Avignon was almost the complete opposite of what I had seen in the front. I walked up the steps of what looked like a tower or fort, and there was a nice, spacious park. The park looks above different parts of the area and, instead of just residential streets, there was a river and some green hills. From there I could see the Pont D'Avignon, officially named the Pont Saint Bénezet. Aside from the amazing historic aspect of the site, the view was breathtaking from almost any angle. I was astonished that you could have a basic city setting on one side of a town and then walk a little farther and the other half be beautiful open land. I took this as a lesson to make sure I research and explore even more when I'm in a new city.

I was beginning to get into better shape for basketball as I logged more practices with the team. These practices helped me to understand the way the game is played in France, and also to get to know the team more. Unfortunately, the team had already called up another foreign player before my arrival, so it looked like they would not be able to sign me to a contract. A few of the players were more disappointed than I was, but I was glad that I had initiated some sort of relationship with the club. One of my teammates was a brother from Sweden named Raphael. He had a few connections and forwarded them to me with the hope that I would find a team, because he was confident in my skills. I did not exactly know where I was headed next, but I decided I would get a few more practices in with the team to make sure I was in shape.

CHAPTER 9

Dreams in Girona

I had spent one month in Girona, Spain the prior year, only returning to see if I had arrived at a better time to get signed by a team. I arrived in February during the prior season, so I figured a team would be likelier to pick me up since it was now the beginning of September. Before I went to any basketball combine academies, I chose to visit a couple of teams in the area to see if they were open to giving me a workout like I had had in Avignon. I had a solid knowledge of quality Spanish teams, and I knew which ones I wanted to play for. I had always heard of Tarragona, Spain, and I knew of a couple Americans who had played for teams there. After my small success in Avignon, I knew that it was in my best interest to speak to the team myself and see if it was possible for me to help them. I had let people speak for me before in the capacity of agent, but I was not too satisfied with the results.

Tarragona struck me as a calm and relaxed city, but it still had nice boardwalks and a colorful personality to it. I only booked an apartment for a couple days, because I wanted to know up front if the team would allow me to play. I was not going to waste my time in the city if they weren't. I found an Airbnb not too far from the gym, and I stayed with a small family that had a place along a main avenue. The introduction was extremely difficult, because they barely spoke English and I could hardly understand their Spanish. After working through the language barrier, I got settled in and attempted to get to know the family in a short period of time. My time was limited, so I turned my efforts towards looking for a gym and talking with one of the team officials before the day was done. My calculations about where the gym was located were actually more precise in this city, and I only had to walk down a few streets to talk to the team.

Walking in this part of Spain was a different experience for me, because drivers yield to people in the street, but I was still constantly hesitant. By growing up in Philadelphia, I learned that assuming you have the right away in any scenario is a poor idea, and you need to make eye contact with a driver before walking across the street. I made it to the arena, and the gym was fairly nice. I thought I could see myself playing there. I had previously asked the family for the proper questions to ask in Spanish to indicate that I was looking for the coach or president. I stumbled through the translation, but everybody understood enough and pointed me in the right direction.

By this point in my basketball team search, talking to team officials and coaches no longer made me nervous or scared. I knew that I could play, and I was confident in my ability to help any team that was looking to win a championship. All I needed was one chance to prove myself and the rest would take care of itself. The coach was not at the gym, but there was an assistant. I gave him my story, along with my practice proposal. He said that the team had just gotten a verbal offer from an American and they had reached their limit on foreigners. I countered by pointing out him that I was there in person and I should at least be able to practice with the team to see if I was a good fit. The assistant called the coach and the coach said that the practice they were going to have that night revealed too much strategy, and he did not want to give that information up. I felt as if he was simply brushing me off, but the assistant did tell me to send my highlight video over and he would contact me if he needed to.

I honestly thought about showing up to the practice anyway, and I believe that I should have, now that I think back on it. I didn't, however, because at that time I was so confident in my game that I wanted to play for a team that was open-minded enough to give me a shot. Now that I had finished my goal of talking with a team, I wanted to see what the city of Tarragona was like and if there were any nice restaurants that I might like. Tarragona has the look of most towns in Catalonia, but the business developers did a great job with the tourist avenues and walkways. The city of Tarragona reminds me of a small Barcelona, but the feeling is more intimate and personal. It has some attributes of a big city, but the "rat race" atmosphere isn't present, and that's what makes it so special.

One major problem that I have with Europe is the hours when stores are open and how restaurants serve food around these times. Any hunger from 4 to 6 PM is a serious problem, because you may travel around for a long time in search of an open restaurant. This issue becomes even more prominent if you are selective (like me) when choosing where to dine. This section of Spain is also heavily into preserved pig legs, called Iberian ham, which are a huge turnoff to my appetite. I do not eat pork anymore, but I'm still not sure if Iberian ham is something I would call a treat, even if I still did. I may have walked around for an hour and made three trips around the neighborhood before I found something I liked.

I found a well-designed Italian restaurant that was completely empty, but the menu was interesting. At the time, I was working on changing my diet and trying more vegetables, so I thought the grilled vegetables as a starter would be helpful. After years and years of fried squid as an appetizer at Italian restaurants, I was finally making a change for the better. Once I tasted the vegetable platter, I began to understand why I might have not ordered vegetables much in the States. Though the vegetables were grilled, I could still taste the freshness, and the vinaigrette was rich and far from cheap. My mind started to wonder if it was not my taste or desires that were the problem, but the lack of quality in America. This restaurant was not the top of the line in Spain, but it was still highly respectable and affordable. The quality was far superior than the type of meal you could find in a chain restaurant back home, so I was beginning to see the differences in standards.

Throughout my travels, my diet consistently took a serious hit every time I tasted the freshness of a different city. Once you get exposed to natural tastes and dishes that have been carefully prepared, your taste is forced to change. I do not remember the name of the Italian entrée I ordered, but it was sautéed chicken in a tomato sauce, and it was second to none. This restaurant looked like it was not sure if it wanted to be a chain or an authentic mom and pop restaurant. The design may have been off, but all of the food I tasted had an authentic touch, and the service was wonderful. Back home in America, I might have had to pay fifty dollars in total for much smaller portions, so I was happy that this place was not too outrageous in their prices.

When I walked back through the city, I noticed that even though I was not fond of the city's restaurants, their sorbet options were plentiful, and I was unsuccessful in my efforts to avoid them. I do not indulge in dessert much, but I've always been used to cheap water ice, with its high fructose corn syrup, so sorbet is something I find difficult to turn down. Tarragona hadn't gone the way I planned, but I still ended my time there with a delicious sorbet and a walk through the city on a summer night.

I began to sense that the pre-season had already started and most teams had their rosters set up. I had the feeling that most teams weren't currently looking for Americans outside of their sports agent connections, so I had to make some quick decisions. I decided to go back to the basketball academy in Girona, Spain, to see what my chances were of finding a team to pick me up. I also thought it was a great idea to go back so I could practice five times a week and stay in shape, effectively killing two birds with one stone. The academy had gone through some slight changes since the last time I was there, but I was fine with them, because I knew my time there would only be temporary. This Girona trip was different than the first time I had gone, because I knew what to expect, and I was not going to be too picky about what team situations I put myself into.

The first time I went to the academy, I had made some great friendships with guys I played with, and we also won games that we weren't expecting to. From those relationships, I was able to see other people realize their dreams and goals. From there, I was able to see that it's truly a gift to have the dream of playing sports, and it's not one that should be taken for granted. One of the things that a lot of us had in common was that we came from different sections of the US where some guys our age do not have an outlook and a lot of situations seem hopeless. I felt like our motivation and stories enabled us to sharpen each other. Unfortunately, that was the year before, and I was not looking for those type of friendships this time around. I was only focused on showcasing my talent, and hopefully moving on to a team shortly after arriving there. I would never be arrogant or act like I was untouchable, but I feel like some guys go to another country and have the mindset that they will just hang out and fake it until they make it. I had no intentions of getting caught up in that type of thinking.

The practices weren't much different, but the competition was not as strong as the last time I was there. The great thing was that everyone still had the same determination and most of the guys seemed focused. I spent a couple of days hanging with a few of the guys, going through the usual LeBron James arguments and such. The director of the camp was generous enough to allow me to stay at an apartment away from the usual place that the other players were staying, which was a blessing. Since I had my own apartment, this was an opportunity for me to cook for myself while outside of the US. The apartment was set up nicely, and more importantly, I had my own space.

One meaningful conversation I had was with a couple of guys who weren't from the US. I noticed a pattern where they were getting picked by teams before the Americans. I do not feel that I am qualified to describe the ways that the foreign recruitment works, but I did find out that it's easier to get picked up if you have something other than a US passport. There was also a guy who had citizenship with Jamaica and he obtained it through descent because his parents were actually born there. My great-grandfather was from Jamaica, so I thought that I should explore the process of obtaining the citizenship if I wanted to make this process easier. I've always identified with Jamaica as my heritage, but I had never known that I could get citizenship through descent. I also identify as Bajan, with my great-grandmother being born in Barbados and relocating to New York. I identify with both countries equally, but Barbados' Department of Citizenship was clear that it would be impossible for me to gain citizenship through descent from Barbados. Whatever the case, I planned on getting picked up by a team regardless of what country's passport I had, so I figured any kind of descent citizenship option would just be a bonus.

I'm not sure why I never had the desire to leisurely walk around while in the States, but I enjoyed walking anywhere and everywhere in Europe. Whether it's through a park, the city, or in a neighborhood, I saw Girona as an easy place to walk around. My apartment and downtown Girona were separated by a small wooded area and park, and I saw that as a great opportunity to explore it a bit and enjoy the scenery. Downtown Girona reminds me of a town in Italy, with its old village design and great restaurants. It is well designed even though it can feel like a maze, and I enjoyed walking aimlessly through the streets as the sun set. There are bridges that give you a great perspective from one side of the city. There is a river that runs through part of the city, even though it isn't always filled with water. Along both sides of the river are houses and business that are colorful and stylish.

Now that I had an apartment to cook in, it was time to start building butcher and grocer relationships. Yet another chance to mispronounce words and have no idea how to ask questions, but this time in a different language. I thought that the conversations I had would run more smoothly if I studied the names of animals before I went to the butcher, looking for a specific cut. After a brief Spanish lesson, I walked over to the stores and, of course, everyone was a little surprised when they saw a Black man. I noticed that they weren't even speaking the type of Spanish that we're used to hearing in America, but instead the language of Catalan. Castilian Spanish is the most commonly spoken in Spain, while Catalan is the regional language of Catalonia. The first time I went to the butcher, there was a lady in line who noticed that I couldn't speak much Spanish or Catalan, so she decided to help me out with the words and pronunciations of my desired food.

Everybody was so nice to me when I went to order at the butcher, which caused me to start to change my initial reservations about people. It made me think back to my own hometown of Philadelphia, when there were some rumblings years back about foreigners ordering cheesesteaks. There was a big complaint about foreigners not being able to speak clear English when placing their order, and that they needed to work on it before buying food at a certain restaurant. I thought about how embarrassed I would be if I was singled out because I wanted to order some food, but I cannot speak a second language that well. I also thought of how sad that story was, that somebody wanted to spend their eight dollars on a single, greasy cheesesteak, and they caught flak because they couldn't order clearly enough. That's the intriguing part about traveling—you learn about what other people have to go through every day when they come to America looking for a new chance. I have a strong respect for people who try to speak a second language, especially those who have gotten themselves jobs that require them to do so.

I know "mis verduras" (my vegetables) in Spanish pretty well, because I remember those food lessons from Spanish class in high school. Anybody who was in my high school Spanish class from sophomore year knows we did not spend much time learning anything, but I remember the pictures of fruits and vegetables and their names, at least. My trip to the grocery store was less eventful, but I did make a discovery that was life-changing. I got my usual favorites and when I went home to cook a dish called saltado de pollo, I noticed that I had made a small mistake. I intended to buy a lime, but when I sliced it open, I realized that the insides were orange. I had no idea what it was, but I decided I would taste it to see if it could be added to my dish. The taste was half orange and half lime and it was the greatest piece of fruit I've ever tasted. I had no idea that there was actually a sweet and sour fruit out there that is also fairly cheap. If they had this fruit back in the states, there would be no need for candy. The next time I went back to the store, I pleaded for the owner to tell me the name of the fruit that I had bought the last time. She said it was a mandarina, which I figured was a mandarin orange, but you could only get them green in that area of Spain around Late August through September. I'm not sure how much money I spent on mandarinas while I was there, but I haven't felt the need to spend money on candy again.

As I settled into Girona, we had a couple of games against local teams and also some games between ourselves so we could get some game film recorded for future use. I did not care about film, because I already had some from the last time I was there, and I just wanted to make sure I pushed to find a team to pick me up. After a couple of games, I learned that there was a team that was interested in me, and, even better, it was located directly next to Barcelona. At this point, the two practices a day, without an adequate weight room, and no championship to win, started to push me towards going with the team. However, I had to be patient and go see the team first, to make sure it was the right fit. I got on the train to a town right outside of Barcelona called Badalona. I met with the coach, who explained that they had a spot open due to injuries.

I arrived at the gym, and it was the exact type of gym that I dreaded playing in. I did not care that the building was old, but the hardwood floor was the type that you might find in on old shack, beat up with scratchy paint. Instantly turned off, I knew they did not have any money to offer me, so figured I would only go to practice and go back to Girona. I did not read about this story until later, but I once read about a former NBA player going to a team overseas, and then seeing the gym and refusing to play there because the quality standards were too low. Had I read that story back then, I may have followed suit and demanded that I play in better conditions.

Later that night when I came back for the actual practice, I was fairly early and did not see any of the coaches or players. I met the janitor and the president of the club simultaneously, and neither spoke English. It did not help that I did not know much Spanish. Back then, I did not even have enough Spanish to say, "I need to change my clothes." We spent a good five minutes trying to understand each other until the president's eight-year-old son came down and translated for me. A group of adults couldn't communicate, but a child had the key, because he spoke great English and was happy to help out. I took that as sign from God that I needed to take my language studying seriously for the future. Later that night, the president walked me towards my apartment and I figured it would be awkward because we could barely communicate. But, I found out that he spoke French, and my French was good enough for us to have a solid conversation about the future of the team.

Practice the next day went well, and it honestly did feel good to actually play with a team because it felt like we were working towards something. During my stay, we played against a higher level team in the preseason and beat them easily. I was able to show that I was an elite defender in a short amount of time. The next game, I did not play at all, and we wound up losing to a team that was on the same level as us.

When I got back to Girona on the weekend, I realized that I was basically being forced to make a decision, because two other guys had moved into the apartment, and their hygiene standards were sub-par. I tried for one day, but there was no way I could stay in that apartment when it looked like a biohazard. I got my bags and headed to Badalona, figuring that things would be looking up since I was basically going to be living in Barcelona.

CHAPTER 10

Life in Barcelona

When I first came to Badalona to visit the team, I stayed with two coaches of the sports club's younger teams. The apartment was a bachelor pad, but I only cared about having a place to sleep in between practices. These gentlemen did not know me from a can of paint, but they welcomed me into their home and showed me great hospitality. The apartment was in the busy section of Badalona, and it was only a few blocks from the beach. By staying with the two coaches, I was able to see how many things there are to do in the region. Badalona is only a subway train ride away from Barcelona, a short walk to the beach, or a hike to the hills. I made sure to enjoy all of these features during my time there, and they strengthened my appreciation for the city.

One of my roommates was a coach for the top team in the city, which played in the highest division in Spain. He offered, unprompted, to give me a tour of La Penya, the home of Joventut Badalona. It's also a historical building, because this is the same place that Michael Jordan and the Dream Team played when they played in the 1992 Barcelona Olympics. I was thankful that God opened this avenue for me, because this was ultimately the level that I wanted to reach. How ironic was it that I was able to see what the top talent looked like as soon as I arrived in Badalona.

The outside of the gym did not look like it had been updated since the Olympics, but it was in far better shape than most places after the Olympics are finished. Even still, I was amazed at how great this arena was and by its location in the middle of this town, away from the big stage in Barcelona.

The inside of the arena had the real look of a professional club and I knew that this was going to be a level that I had to work hard to reach. The team's practice did not look very strenuous, but I did notice that the system and strategy was more detailed and crisp than anything I had seen during my time in Europe. I guess God was trying to show me that I was so close, but still so far. I now had the vision of what the top level was and what to expect. Later that night, I went back to my own team's practice focused and prepared to attack all my goals. I tried not to focus on the difference in gyms and situations, but they were hard to ignore, and the most obvious differences weren't necessarily physical or aesthetic.

Once I filled out my paperwork to sign with the team, I was told that I would be staying with an assistant manager's family for a month, while my own apartment situation was being handled. At first I was shocked that a family was willing to take in some random Black man from America—for no less than an entire month. I was looking forward to staying at their apartment in Barcelona, but I wondered if they would be able to handle me living there. However, as it turned out, my stay with the family was never awkward or strange at any time, because they treated me like I was their family from start to finish. They extended their hospitality as if I were the top scorer in the NBA and they had to show me a good time so that I would sign to their team. The father was kind enough to show me their neighborhood of Poblenou. The "barrio" is very close to the beach and you can walk on the boardwalk right into the downtown tourist sections of the city. This was definitely a different setting, but surely one that I could get used to.

Initially, the language barrier was a small problem, but I made sure to study Spanish every night, because I think it's in poor taste to make someone cater to you in their own country. I took this as a great opportunity to learn Spanish and understand what phrases are commonly used. The complete family consisted of the father, mother, a son, and a daughter, but the daughter was living in Madrid at the time. I spent most of my time studying and touring the city while the family was at work or school during the day. They were generous enough to cook for me if I needed them to, but the mother said she did not cook much and I was happy to tell her that she did not have to worry about me. Catalonians have a very interesting take on cuisine, and to this day, I am not sure if their take agrees with my taste. Even though the American burger and fries does not give my perspective much credibility, I still get puzzled when my friends post their Catalan dishes.

I did not have much of an issue going to the butcher, but buying poultry or lamb from the supermarket was a bit problematic for me. The family assured me that there weren't antibiotics and steroids in the food like you might find in the USA. I tried to convince myself of this fact, but most of the time I ended up paying that extra euro for a package of chicken that weighed less, just to get that certified sticker saying that it was organic. The family always treated me well, and the father was a true man of respect, always making sure that I was okay. If there were nights where I was in the living room studying on my computer, he would hang out and talk to me to make sure I did not have to feel alone. My Spanish improved as we watched pro European basketball games together. I would usually complain about how the referees do not give any calls to the Americans on either team, but that's for a different book. I was continually amazed at how well I was treated by strangers during my time in Europe. By the end of my stay with the family, my Spanish was coming to me a little faster, and I was beginning to understand them a lot easier.

I was still practicing at this time, but I was not able to play because my paperwork was still processing. Our record was 3-1 before I was cleared to start playing, so I figured that there was no way we would lose a game if I played at all. My apartment situation was moving very slow, as the coach had forgot to look for one, and it was almost time for me to leave the family's apartment. It was great staying with the family and learning from them, but as a man, I was ready to have my own apartment and get into my comfort zone. I decided to look for myself and see if there were some places that would be a good fit for me. During this chaos, my paperwork cleared, and I was determined to take the team from a contender to the clear favorite. I had a lot more energy and motivation in practice, and I couldn't wait to destroy the opponent in the next game.

The coach told me he found an apartment not far from the gym, and we went to meet the owner before a practice to hash out the details. We went into a random building in Badalona and entered a basic apartment with a nice lady who began to speak Spanish with my coach. The place was clean, but I was only going to have one room to myself. At this point, I did not really care—I was just ready to play basketball, and I would stay there until I could find something better. The lady spoke French, so we were able to agree on the amount and when she would get the money. Shortly after the agreement, my coach said something to her in Spanish, and suddenly the whole vibe of the conversation went downhill. She went from being kind and soft-spoken to furious, saying that the deal was off and there was no possible way that I could stay there. Until this day, I do not know what he said, but I know that although we had a deal in French, something went terribly wrong in Spanish. What appeared to be nothing more than a formality was now nothing at all.

I had to leave the Poblenou apartment because the family's daughter was coming back in town for a while and they needed that space. Regardless, opening your house to a grown man that you do not know should have a month limit, anyway! The president of the team gave me a few days at a hotel by the beach to figure out my living situation. The hotel was lacking in any luxury, but it was in a great location, looking right at the Balearic Sea. I spent much time on the sand, relaxing and just enjoying the opportunity I had, and all the possibilities for the future. The boardwalk along the coast served as an easy way to clear my head, also.

I knew the decision would be left up to me, so I decided to book an Airbnb after I left the hotel. While all of this was going on, I got some disturbing news that somebody that I considered close enough to be a family member had passed away. Errol was like a big cousin to me and had welcomed me into his group of cousins like I was his family. The fact that I had recently seen him at another family member's funeral and talked about life was even more difficult. It was clear from that point that this season was going to be a mission and I was going to dedicate my play to Errol. So, of course, there was no chance that my team was going to lose when I played, and people would most likely fear my intensity.

I didn't play much in the first game that I was eligible, but it was great chance for me to evaluate where I was physically and mentally. I was so thirsty to play that I began anticipating what everybody was going to do with the ball before they even made a move. The more my competitive spirit took over, the more the coaching staff was able to understand me. After the first game, I realized that the coaches wanted me to keep that same energy in practice. I pride myself on always giving 150% with anything I do, but our practices never had the energy or seriousness to motivate my competitive side. Part of this was that we had a rather young team, and even the older guys on the team were relaxed in practice. It also didn't help that our gym had one of the worst wooden floors in Spain, so I definitely wasn't planning on injuring myself. Sections of the court would frequently be cautioned with a cone because of a roof leak whenever it rained. Even though conditions worsened throughout the winter when I found out that there wasn't a heating system in the gym, I still made it in for voluntary morning shooting practice several times a week.

The next Airbnb apartment was across the street from a shopping center and about a twenty minute walk from the gym. I usually do not stay with anyone when I rent an Airbnb, but I needed to buy time and did not want to pay too much money while I was barely going to be there anyway. The apartment was nice, but there were way too many people there when I arrived. It was like a breakfast party when I got there, so I was turned away from the entire situation and started looking for my next apartment the moment I left.

During extended travel, one thing that you may be faced with is finding the middle ground between cost-efficient living and comfort. After bouncing between multiple apartments of varied quality, a previous Airbnb owner contacted me and offered a living space at an reasonable price. The apartment sat behind a nice open park and was a straight shot down a major avenue to get to the team gym. I enjoyed the neighborhood of Montigala because it had a shopping center, parking lot, and also was not too far from the train station. The walk down the hill to practice was therapeutic and scenic, but some nights the walk back up the hill after practice was laborious. It was amusing that I basically had to walk by that Olympic arena on my way to my team's gym almost every day. I took that as a sign that my goal was not too far away, and I was motivated to keep working hard to get there. The walk got more difficult as autumn transitioned into winter, so I was thankful when I got a ride from my teammate, Pedro, from time to time.

Although I was beginning to see Barcelona as my home, I still liked to appease my tourist side and check out the city's landmarks some days. My other teammate, Brian, was from the States, and his sister was in town and wanted to go to Sagrada Familia, a church famous for its detailed design. After seeing the Great Pyramids of Giza, most man-made buildings do not really intrigue me, but I thought that it might make a good day trip. One thing I did like about Sagrada Familia was the sculptures, and how they told a story of the scriptures in the Bible. Some of the scenes were easily recognizable, but there were some that I had to look up in the Bible for understanding. Most of Sagrada Familia is well designed and sophisticated, but I think there's a lot of money that is wasted at the site. I have always believed that church is a place for worship and fellowship, and all of the bells and whistles distract from the true meaning. They said that the church will not be finished for a long time, and I think it's a waste of good money that could have gone to a charitable cause.

It was great to have some family and friends come to Barcelona. I had received word that my Hampton University buddy, Blake, was coming to Barcelona to host a party somewhere in the city. It had been a while since I had been to LA to see all my friends, so it was going to be great to get a chance to hang out with my friends abroad. I did not go to clubs at all during my time in Barcelona, because I usually only go out with friends that I trust. Although my basketball practices always went late, it just so happened that when practice was over around 11 PM, I was able to get a ride into Barcelona from one of the assistant coaches. The restaurant/club bouncers had a problem at the door because I was dressed casually and I also had my gym bookbag with me. I told them that I was only here because my friend was hosting the party, and they could just call him over. After Blake and the promoter came outside, the problem was rectified, and I entered the well designed and exclusive restaurant.

It was good to catch up with him, talk about old times, and look forward to the future. I had never been in the type of setting where you sit down at the restaurant and then all of a sudden the club basically starts and everyone heads to the dance floor. I guess all my nights staying away from clubs got rolled into one because the company gave Blake V.I.P. status, complete with a couple bottles of Dom Perignon. Blake was doing his usual—getting the crowd hyped and controlling the flow—meanwhile I was mellow and relaxed like I usually am after practice. I did network a little and make small talk, but it was mostly fake love, because we were in the V.I.P. section. It was a great night, but it's not something I can do often, because my body was in pain the next day. It reminded me of my time in Los Angeles when I was being dragged to a different venue every other night by my buddies, and the next morning would arrive before I went to sleep. But no matter what part of the world I'm in, it's imperative that I link up with my friends if we are in the same city. It's great to visit these amazing cities and countries when you are traveling solo, but it's far better when you can share it with someone from back home.

My team was on a winning streak and at the top of the division, now that I had started playing. My dad wanted to come to

Barcelona to check out a game and maybe visit another city in Spain. Once he arrived in Barcelona, I realized that I was in full European mode because I noticed that he was not used to walking so much. I've always found it easier to walk off a meal in Europe than in the US because the portions are usually different. and many Americans do not go for a walk after eating. It was now December, and the gym was freezing cold. Since our team did not believe in heat for practice, I'm sure my Dad was uncomfortable watching. The game was much warmer for me, because the body heat from the spectators helped with the temperature, and my adrenalin was pumping anyway. This was against our rival, Boet Mataro, the second best team in the division, so it helped that the stands were filled to capacity.

The challenge of facing another good team with a couple of Americans on it had me on a mission to prove that I was the best US import of the year. The game was so intense that I never got tired, and I was able to react to any play offensively or defensively. The point guards and shooting guards on my team had more of a shoot the ball first mentality, so that didn't leave many shots for me as a forward. As a result, the opposing team must have figured that I couldn't shoot, and they gave me a lot of space on my first time touching the ball. I'm not sure how far behind the 3 point line I was, but there was nobody in front of me. I immediately fired up a shot, and it hit the backboard and went in. I laughed it off as a lucky shot, but I hoped that they continued to doubt my shooting ability. My team's assistant coach told me later on that the coach yelled in Spanish, "Back up, he can't shoot!" I didn't do much to prove him wrong, but the shot went in.

Defensively, I was everywhere, and I made a huge impact, even though I feel like I was called for some seriously bogus fouls (I have footage of the game if you don't believe me). Even though I fouled out late in the game, I still had my best game overall, and my team won rather easily.

The win carried us into a holiday break, and we had a couple of extra days off from practice. I noticed that there are a lot of holidays in Spain and France. I guess that since the history of Spain and France goes back way farther than the USA, there are more things to acknowledge. Nonetheless, it seems like stores are on a holiday schedule every ten days. I was able to use these free days to travel to Toledo, Spain, with my father, where I had heard about the Maghrebi traveling through and leaving a heavy influence. Toledo is located just a short train ride away from Madrid, but it's completely different from the big city. The first noticeable characteristic of the city is the layout, which appears to be built on and in between a bunch of hills. The very fact that someone was able to make a picturesque city out of the terrain is impressive. My hotel was located at one of the highest points, which allowed for a great view of the city, as well as the sunrises and sunsets. Between my hotel and the city, I felt like I had a mix between a log cabin getaway and a small town. It was in the perfect position to allow me to go on a hike, but also journey through the different parts of the city if I chose to.

Toledo is a major city where the Maghrebi (Moors) came through from Africa and left a lot of visual treasures and customs. Most of their architecture and influence is extensively visible throughout the city. The Spanish-African mixture is one of the attributes that sets Toledo apart from the bigger cities of Spain. Toledo was very much a history lesson about migration and the different rulers who came through Spain. Much of the architecture, food, and music that is known to many areas stem from the mixture of cultures. I went into a few museums and was impressed by the great designs, but I was also disappointed that there was no real mention of the Maghrebi anywhere. My favorite building was the Santa Maria La Blanca Synagogue, which was meticulously designed and crafted. It was amazing that these small cities could bring out so many people, and that the streets could be so crowded on a December night.

When I got back to Badalona, the owner of the apartment let me know that someone was going to be moving into the room in January and basically my days in Badalona were numbered. I honestly took this as a sign from God, meaning that it was time to move on and find a better situation somewhere else. The team was winning, but the facility was not allowing me to reach my full potential because the weight room was lacking in quality equipment and the gym was far too cold to get a great workout in. From a professional standpoint, it was an easy decision, but I did feel bad that I would have to tell my teammates and other friends that my journey was headed in a different direction. I had done Paris already, so I was not too eager to jump back into that life, especially during the winter. I decided to take some time to think about where I was going to go and how I was going to accomplish the goals that I'd set.

At this point, we were still on a break from any games or much practice, but my teammates did invite me to play in a 3-on-3 tournament. I usually don't play in these types of tournaments, because I like running up and down the court. After declining the invite several times, I finally agreed and joined a team with the goal of just getting a workout. In the elimination round, we played against a big and strong team who had a center from a higher division in Spain. I took it as an opportunity to prove that I can play at that level, so I was now completely focused on getting the win.

Any type of European tournament without an official league sanctioning it usually has a fast pace. I've concluded that the rules of soccer have influenced the gameplay of other sports in Europe. If the ball goes out of bounds, teams can pick up the ball immediately and inbound to start play again before the opposing team is ready.

Our elimination game had that exact pace and I was really trying to adjust to the rules and make sure I was always aware of the situation. Towards the end of the game, we were trailing by four points and I ran to defend the big center. I stepped on his foot, and amongst all the noise in the gym, I heard a crack from mine. I finished the game, but I got home and had the feeling that it was broken once the adrenalin wore off. I knew I should've stuck with my original decision and skipped the tournament, but I didn't want to come off as an arrogant American. We had practice the next day, and of course there were no taxis or buses going down the main avenue to to the gym at that time. I limped down the hill for about 15 mins before I was able to find a taxi. Interesting enough, the entire team was either sick, injured, or away with their family, so we only had game film for practice.

I got an evaluation by the team trainer and he said that there wasn't anything broken and should be fine in a few weeks. The foot was still difficult to walk on, but he assured me that I wouldn't be walking much at all if it was broken. Sure enough, my foot gradually got better and I was able to start practicing again. We were on a long break, so it was doubtful that I would miss any games. Regardless, I was just thankful that my foot wasn't broken and it wouldn't jeopardize any plans I had of making it to a higher division of basketball in Europe.

My Mom and my sister Joy made a timely last-minute decision to come visit me for Christmas. I knew this was going to be an interesting trip, because they are "off the wall" in America, and I could only imagine what would happen in Barcelona. They stayed close to the Goth section in Barcelona, which is a main tourist area, so I always met up with them to walk through the city. Barcelona is a place where Americans can walk forever and sightsee, so we enjoyed a great number of miles together. We had a healthy balance of exploring the city and looking for restaurants that had delicious menus. We found a Peruvian restaurant that had the best food I have ever tasted in Barcelona. The fish ceviche was a great set up for the Peruvian chicken with crisp seasoning. The theme of the week was to look for ethnic restaurants, because it was obvious that they were of high quality in Barcelona. The only thing that I sat out was a gospel music concert that Joy and my Mom went to at the Palau de la Musica Catalana. I'm sure the performance was highly entertaining, but I can only take so much tourism in a week.

Christmas was a great time with Joy and my mother, and after a long search that day, we found a downtown rooftop restaurant that was open. For whatever reason, my team had an extensive break throughout the new year, so I had a lot of time to spend with my family. It was a huge boost having family come visit me because I got to laugh like my true self. Many of the Barcelonans got to see how funny we were as a group, also. Of course, Joy had to ruin the great trip by crying like a baby when it was time for them to leave and go to the airport. They tried to drive me crazy, but we still had a wonderful time, and it prepared me for my next move to France.

After my family left, I had about another week in Barcelona, and my team had a tournament to play against a few teams that were in a higher division. My foot wasn't 100 percent, but I felt invincible, because I was finally getting used to the gameplay in Spain. I was finally in the starting lineup, and I was so focused defensively that I had about four steals to begin the first game. The opposing team had some skilled players, however, and were also a little taller than us. We won the game on a buzzer beater by our oldest veteran, Jose Luis. The whole team rushed the court and celebrated with cheers in Spanish. We won the subsequent championship game easily and I began to see a pattern where I always play at a higher level when I play against a higher division. I convinced myself that it made sense to search for a higher level team to play for. This journey was about challenging myself, and I figured that was a sign that I was making the right move and should demand more for myself. I made up my mind to tell the team I was leaving during the transition to the second part of the season. I'm not sure if the other teams were surprised that we won the tournament, but I knew we were the best team from the start. During my time with the team, I played in fourteen wins and zero losses. I was sure that we could win the championship if I stayed, but I knew it was time to move on. My coaches and teammates were disappointed that I had to go, but they understood that I had to find a better situation.

CHAPTER 11

A Resident in Toulouse

The unforgettable trips that I had made to Paris and Nice in the past gave me a ton of confidence that I would be able to live almost anywhere in France. I knew that Toulouse was most likely nothing like Paris, but as long as they had baguettes and a basketball gym, I felt that I should be fine. I was glad that Toulouse would not be as frigid as Paris in the winter, but the cold was still present when I arrived. Toulouse and Barcelona are only about 4 hours apart driving, but the climates are completely different in the winter, even with Barcelona being next to the water. In France, the sun can be clear in the sky, but it's so cold that it feels like it's there for light purposes only. Once I landed in Toulouse, I thought about taking public transportation to get to my Airbnb apartment, but I decided it would be smartest and warmest to take an Uber.

The neighborhood where I was staying was still inside the city limits, but close enough to the suburbs where it looked like your typical French suburban neighborhood. I chose an apartment that appeared to be close enough to the gym that I could walk back and forth throughout the day. From a cost-efficient standpoint, the apartment was also more spacious and affordable than a place you might find in the center of the city. I did my usual walk through the neighborhood to see what supermarkets, butcheries, and bakeries were close to my apartment. My new neighborhood was called Barriere De Paris, and business-wise, it was well planned, with a few choices of supermarkets in any direction I walked and a metro station and buses that went into the city. I was surprised to find that there was also a fitness gym not far from my apartment, which meant I now I had easy access to the weight room and the basketball gym.

I thought it would be a great idea to get a look at downtown Toulouse on my first night, so I could get an idea of the city. Since there was a Cowboys-Packers playoff football game on back in the States, I found a bar that was showing the game until they closed. Aside from daylight savings time, France is usually six hours ahead of standard Eastern time, so it's rare that I ever catch any primetime matchups. This Cowboys-Packers playoff game seemed like it was perfectly timed for me, and it would be ending as soon as the bar closed. Once I walked into the bar and the bartender spoke to me, I realized I had lost my French rhythm. Even up until the writing of this book, I'm still getting comfortable with speaking French, but my time in Paris had at least helped me gain a rhythm with my conversations. Once the gentleman started talking to me, the words weren't firing off in my brain like they usually do. I'm sure it had to do with my time in Spain and learning the conversational language there. The bartender began to realize that my French was horrible and used what English he knew to let me know the NFL game was on in the back. The game turned out to be a great ending, with the Cowboys losing because of a last second field goal right as I was about to leave the bar.

Just like my time in Spain, I did not consider my stay in Toulouse to be a vacation. I immediately made sure to set up all my memberships so I could get right into the flow of basketball life. I Googled the walking path to the gym from the apartment, and it turned out to be a 45-minute walk instead of the 20 minutes that I had imagined. Once again, my brief research failed me, and it was possible that I would have to explore options other than walking. By traversing the surrounding neighborhoods, I was able to see how low-key this section of Toulouse was. It was evident that there were plenty of opportunities there for business development in the near future. While I noticed that I would have to walk across a bridge to get outside the city limits, I became anxious to see just how far this trip that I planned on taking would be.

The walk was a true 45 minutes, and felt even longer due to the winter and lack of proper sidewalks provided. My arrival at the gym felt like home because the setup was much like the location in Paris, maybe even better. Since the gym was well designed and allowed more sunlight to shine through it, I was glad that I'd be able to spend time alone there. The director at this location was also an African brother, and his introduction was very professional. He introduced himself as Muz, and he immediately understood that my French was not perfect and that he would have to utilize his English. The difference between the Toulouse gym and the one in Paris was that the Toulouse gym's lobby area layout and the surrounding neighborhood were far more welcoming. I noticed that there were very few people there at 10 AM like in Paris, but everyone seemed to pour in from noon to 2 PM.

I began to realize that the work schedules are far different than the system that we have in the States. Our system in the US gives us about thirty minutes to an hour of break time for lunch, and we use that to get something to eat. I usually worked out from 9 AM to 2 PM, and I noticed that Toulousains in the workforce might get off at lunch and go shoot hoops for a little over an hour before going back to finish out the work day. I know there are some who do the same in the USA, but the lunch break schedules in France are far more relaxed than our labor-focused schedules in America. In Paris, the people with basketball gym memberships were usually my age or younger, but rarely older than me, like they were in Toulouse. That observation alone allowed me to see the difference in customs for certain parts of France.

After a few days of working out, I began to feel comfortable with the city and felt the need to spend some time exploring it. After walking through Toulouse, it became obvious to me that France specializes in creating perfect settings for long walks. Toulouse is much smaller than Paris, but there are still plenty of different areas that you can walk through and enjoy the fresh air. I spent a considerable amount of time looking for various butchers and bakeries, but also for the many street markets. One small culture shock that I encountered in France after staying in Spain was the amount of Africans that I saw. I honestly was not sure if the diversity of France was just a Parisian thing, but after my time in Toulouse, I realized that there's a significant African presence even outside of Paris.

The only drawback to my apartment was that it did not have any wireless internet. Therefore, I had to look for alternatives to get some of my missions completed. It turned out to be a positive setback, because I was forced to get out of the apartment and go downtown to use the wi-fi at Starbucks or Mcdonald's. The cashiers at Starbucks easily picked up that I was American, and they would let me slide if I used their wi-fi without buying something first. The security guards usually tell you to leave, but these brothers weren't strict like the guards in the Parisian supermarkets. Centre-Ville Toulouse gave me a great idea of how diverse the city is, and I never got the idea that it was something they were trying to hide or weren't proud of. This simple aesthetic observation encouraged me to spend a lot of time in the Capitole area and be amongst the people.

The gym allowed me to meet even more people who were glad to hear that I wanted to play in France. A short African man walked up to me one day while I was shooting in the gym and introduced himself as Coach Aboudou. He said that he was starting an academy in the area with his business partners, Chadi and Arthur, and that he would be able to help me get in shape to play for a French team. The three of us had a small meeting, and they were incredibly proactive with trying to find me the right connections to get onto a team, all while getting their academy off the ground. They suggested that I help out the academy and practice my French while teaching the kids. I already coached basketball back home, so using my spare time to direct French kids and meet new people was no problem. My workouts were becoming redundant, so it served as a great opportunity to get pointers and basketball drills from someone who knew about the French system.

The academy gym was about a half hour outside of Toulouse, in the town of Muret, an affluent area. The kids filed in, and in total there may have been about forty boys and girls present. Coach Aboudou surprised me by telling me to introduce myself to the kids and their parents in French. I was not nervous, but I did not have a lot of confidence in my pronunciations. Everyone said they understood me for the most part, and I was relieved that I did not have to speak for any longer, because I was running out of sentences. It was a helpful test, because after that day, I consistently worked on introducing myself in French and explaining my mission.

The day went well, and a reporter from a newspaper was there to get some information on the academy and also hear about why I was in France. The kids were happy to see an American, and they took every chance they could to use their American street slang they learned from television. I also saw that the basketball learning curve is similar for the kids in France, because they always want to attempt the shots with the highest level of difficulty. Kids who were half my size trying to shoot half-court shots and complete dribbling exhibitions like Steph Curry. The kids would not let me leave until I did an off the backboard dunk while they recorded it on their phones. I'm aware that they could not understand that I was not having an easy transition from coach to player at the age of thirty, but I did it for them anyway.

During my time in Spain and Toulouse, I went through a serious diet change, focusing more on stews and raw foods than my usual sautéed dishes that used olive oil heavily. I suppose the change was necessary, because it provided more energy to play basketball at my age as well as helping in terms of everyday health. The variety of markets that carry vegetables and fruits in France makes eating healthily a painless transition, with the added bonus being that they cost less in comparison to the USA. I also decided to focus more on the details of my cooking when I found an old cookbook in the apartment. In the States, you usually have to search far and wide for specific ingredients for "haute cuisine," but in France, you can most likely find them in your neighborhood supermarket.

For example, I was in a basic chain supermarket named Casino and they had morilles mushrooms that I had a hard time finding back home. I saw Gordon Ramsay do a sauce with the mushrooms once, and he says they take the sauce to another level. The price tag was pretty steep, with a 25 gram jar costing 18 Euros, and the more prominent brand costing around 25 euros. Once I incorporated these mushrooms into my chicken gravy, however, it was clear that Gordon Ramsay was telling the truth about their greatness.

Being surrounded by all of these fresh ingredients, groceries, and butcher cuts, I still I had a desire to try the Pizza Hut that was not too far from my apartment. After working out for about five hours, it's difficult to cook every night and not desire a quickly prepared meal. I haven't eaten at Pizza Hut regularly since college because I think they've changed their recipe, but I did want to see if the taste was different in Europe. The first order showed that the dough was far better quality than what you find in the States, but they did not use much tomato sauce, and the cheese was almost solid. So I tweaked my order the next time, saying, "Beaucoup de sauce tomate et un peu de fromage," which meant that I wanted extra tomato sauce and a little bit of cheese, in the hope that that would give me the pizza texture I was looking for. Those small changes got me the best pizza I've had in a while, and I ended up going there a few more times during my stay in Toulouse.

At this point in my journey, I was satisfied with everything I had done in Europe. From actually playing with a team to making French connections and improving my language skills. I was more than ready to go home when my apartment booking was finished, but I continued to hear about the problems back home after the political changes of January 2017. Four different times, family members or friends said that they felt safer if I was in Europe rather than the US. From the outside, it really did look as if the US was divided, and it did not seem safe with all the different conflicts that were arising. I honestly took that as a sign from God that I should stay put and explore what immediate options I had in Toulouse.

I knew I had to leave Europe because my 90-day visa was almost up, and I did not want to test the legal policies. I had to leave for a small period of time before I could come back and stay another 90 days. Africa made the most sense, because I was so close, and I wanted to get back to a warmer climate. My second dilemma was where I would stay in Toulouse when I got back from my travels. I told my basketball academy buddies that I needed to find reasonably priced housing for my return, and my friend Chadi told me that his people would take care of my situation. I thought that would be a difficult task, because I was only going to be gone for about twelve days. I did not know them for long, but something told me that I did not have to worry at all. That's one thing I appreciate about France—when someone says they'll help you out, they genuinely try their best to make it happen for you without conflict.

CHAPTER 12

African Affirmation

By living in different countries, I have had the chance to meet people from all over the world. I've been able to learn about places I would not have ever imagined being able to go. Social media also makes it easier to get an idea of what a country or city may look like and the different things you can experience if you decide to go.

At that time, I followed a lot of Francophone Africans with the hopes of improving my French literacy. I had only heard a little of Dakar, Senegal, but I saw many French-African Instagram travelers going there. It made sense to me that if everyone was going there, it was most likely a delightful place to be. I concluded that this would also give me a chance to hear French as it is spoken in Africa and see if I could get around with my current level in French. One of my teammates in Spain was actually from Senegal, and he would translate the coaches' Spanish directions to French when I couldn't understand well enough, so I felt comfortable with the Senegalese already.

I found a flight that went from Toulouse to Senegal, but there was an overnight layover in Casablanca, Morocco. Being able to see two African cities in one trip would be a bonus, especially because I've heard some good things about Moroccan cuisine. Casablanca isn't Marrakech, but I did not think it could be so different. I found an Airbnb for Dakar, Senegal, and it was close to a couple places, so I figured I could walk or take a short taxi ride to any place that I wanted to go. The room looked nice online, and was rather cheap, so I said I would stay for a week and a half. I had to explore every part of Dakar, because I needed to see what the craze was about. I did my research on Casablanca, Morocco, first and found a restaurant and a couple of landmarks that I could visit during my short stay.

I took a Moroccan airline, and I'm pretty sure that's why one of our stops was in Casablanca. Even while I was on my flight, I was able to witness first-hand that our cultures are quite different. I'm positive that I saw a bunch of no-smoking signs on the plane and the safety video, but the whole flight smelled like the smoking section at a bowling alley. Every time someone went to the bathroom, the smell of burning tobacco became stronger in the main cabin. One positive about the first flight was the lamb dish that was served for the in-flight meal. The dish was a lamb sauce with prunes over rice. I never knew you could use prunes and lamb together, but the taste of the spicy sauce with the sweet prunes was a marvelous combination. This was a dish that I might be cooking for a lifetime. After the smoky flight, I landed in Casablanca and looked for the best traveling options to my hotel, which was near the coast line.

I found out that I had to take a train into the city and then walk a little to get to my hotel. I had no idea what to expect, so, in a sense, I was just going with the flow. The train platform was filled with people who had tons of luggage, and I was not sure if I was going to find a seat on the next train departure. We all boarded the train and I managed to find a seat, and even though it was uncomfortable, I was just looking forward to putting my bags down and seeing Morocco. It occurred to me that I had become naïve, with my newfound European entitlement, to expect the best technology and transportation. The train started moving, and it felt like we were riding on wobbly wheels from 1850. The turns were so sharp and jerky that I thought we were going to fall off the tracks a couple times. Nobody else seemed to be bothered by the uneasy train ride, so I shook it off as "foreigner fear."

Of course, we arrived at the last stop and it was a brand spanking new train station with a Starbucks and Mcdonald's, which appears to be a common combination for any place that I go. If the train station looked this nice, then I knew the tourist section had to look like those pictures that I commonly see of Dubai. My hotel was not a far walk from the station, so I used the Starbucks wi-fi to find the trail to my destination. As soon as I stepped off the station steps, the setting started to change back from the vibe of a highly developed country to one of the third world. The sun had gone down by the time I reached the train station, which meant I was really going to have to pay attention to the streets in order to reach my hotel. I crossed a few major avenues in Casablanca, and it felt like some sort of life and death game that I really had to think out. There was still a big city, downtown type of feel, but it felt like six different Grand Prix races were going in different directions.

Once I made it through my last obstacle, I realized that I was crossing into a more residential section, and I needed to pay attention to people more, just to see if anyone could tell that I was obviously an American. One man was on his phone talking and walked through the busy traffic in his flip flops like he did not have a care in the world. After seeing that, I knew that this was not a place to act like a tourist, and I had to snap back into my Philadelphian mode pretty fast. After a few strolls down some dark streets and going past a couple of packed sports bars showing the local soccer game, I finally found my hotel. I had a fairly easy check-in and left my bags in my room before getting directions to walk to a restaurant I wanted to try out. I decided to follow my own advice and return the way that I had come to the hotel. After reaching the main avenue, the path to the restaurant was a straight shot along the coastline.

The restaurant appeared to be an old military fort that hadn't been changed much to accommodate guests looking to dine. The menu was not what I was expecting, but I still tried a few local dishes and the taste was pretty good. The Moroccan experience that impressed me the most had nothing to do with the food, but the people I was sitting next to. I sat in between a couple and another group of three who were sitting quite close to me. Both women on my right and my left put their purses right next to me, and looked as if they did not have any worries about what type of person I was. This may seem small or irrelevant to some people, but as a Black man from America, this has never happened to me before. I have been to many countries and I often notice people suddenly putting their hands in their pocket or grabbing their purse when they see me walking down the street. This experience made me feel at home in Morocco, and all the aesthetic differences of the city did not matter to me anymore.

After finishing my meal, the digital map on my phone said that it was another quick and easy walk to see the Mosque of Hassan II. I did not know what I was going to be walking into, but it looked rather safe, because the street was along the coast. The area surrounding the restaurant was well lit, but the farther away I was from that area, the darker it got. I crossed the street, because the presence of what looked to be a government office building and some security made me feel safer. Unfortunately, I got too close to the security kiosk and there was a trained German Shepherd dog who let the whole country know that he was not there to be played with. The presence of vicious dogs became a theme as I walked closer and closer to the Mosque, and this inspired me to communicate with the security guards from afar who knew some French.

It's interesting how it seemed like I was walking in a curve, so I never felt like I was getting closer to the mosque by just seeing it. I had to stay cautious a few times, because there were a few people who looked suspicious, and this open area did not have many people walking around. Once I got close to the Mosque, more street lights appeared, and I could see the coast on the right and a neighborhood on the left. It was a bizarre observation when I looked to the left, because I thought I was in back in Philadelphia for a second. There were a few kids playing some game on a small street that looked identical to a small street you might find in North Philly. Even though I had no idea of what or who was in this neighborhood, I felt comfortable after witnessing such a familiar scene, and I took my time walking up to the Mosque.

The Mosque of Hassan II had bright lights, but it was barricaded off because it was well into the night. There were only a few families relaxing on the beach, and it was a rather mellow setting. I took a few photos and gazed at the water for a bit before heading back for a second walking adventure to my hotel. I thought about looking around the downtown section a little more, but I felt like my night had been eventful enough, and another game of "play in traffic" was not a smart decision. There were a few places around my hotel that looked like they might be worth checking out, but I had to worry about being on time for my flight the next afternoon.

The next morning, I went to the free breakfast buffet that was prepared by the hotel, then went on my way to the train station. Once again, I was in that gray area of "kind of on time, but almost late for my flight," so I was a little uneasy about the slow train. The difficult process of buying a ticket during a business morning, when people are trying to get to their office jobs, slowed down the process even more. I got my ticket and realized that they actually did have modern trains in Casablanca, and the new train I was on resembled something that you might find in America. I arrived on time for my flight to Senegal, and after another smoky flight, I was on my way.

As we exited the plane, I noticed who was taking the trip with me. I saw an African soccer team and a couple of tourists who wanted to see the culture, just like me. I helped some girls with their bags, because it seemed like they were struggling a bit. I noticed how the girls and many other people were switching in and out of their languages pretty often. I heard a lot of French and several different African languages that I couldn't make out. These conversations carried up to the customs line, which seemed pretty small compared to the ones in bigger cities. The process to get through customs was extremely slow, but I passed the time by observing everything and everyone around me. I felt like a veteran when it came to traveling to Africa, so I did not worry about having any problems at the customs window.

When I was called up to the window, the agent asked the usual passport questions and what I would be doing while in the country. After giving my tourist spiel, he said that the Airbnb address I gave him was not specific, and I needed to find the correct address. I looked online and tried to call the owner, but I did not have anything sufficient to get through. I did not suspect this was some sort of hustle, because it does makes sense that if you do not have a hotel, then you need to show where you'll be in the city. I kept insisting that the info that I had was the only thing I could produce and he told me that if there was some sort of money I could give, he could see what he could do. I'm not sure if it was my Philly side or my frugal side, but I immediately objected with a face that said "I'm not giving you a penny in any currency, my brother." After seeing my "you must've lost your mind" face, he immediately let me go through with no problems. Yet again, I passed an African customs test. This exam was disguised a little better, but I feel like I passed with flying colors.

Even though I had made it through customs, the agent still may have been right that the address was not specific enough to find the apartment. The second part of the test was waiting for me when I got to the parking lot. It seemed like the drivers had been waiting for me all day. By this time, I was beginning to feel like Africa was my true home because of how comfortable I was with navigating the taxi offers. I took the time to look above it all and just enjoy the beaming sun and the clear blue sky of Africa. After I focused back on my surroundings, I realized that there were a considerable number of drivers in my face looking for my attention. I suppose that I looked lost, because those same African women whose luggage I carried came over to make sure I was OK. One woman was really concerned for my well-being and told me to be careful out here because the city could be dangerous. The ladies waited with me until I found somebody with a phone who could call the apartment owner.

I found a gentleman with a working phone and called the owner for the exact address. After hanging up, he told me the ride would be one Euro, and I was in accordance. He sent me with his assistant driver and we were on our way to central Dakar. This cab ride was just as great as all my other African trips, and I had been looking forward to it. I was amazed that a lot of the people in Dakar looked and dressed like someone I might know back in the states. Aside from anyone in African clothing, a lot of the millennials were dressed like people you might find back in Atlanta. That observation only illuminates my ignorance in being surprised that people weren't dressed in the stereotypical way I had imagined.

The traffic was heavy, and while we were stopped, street salesmen would come near the car to sell whatever goods they had for the day.

After a fairly long ride, we stopped in a neighborhood that had a few paved sidewalks and was a basketball court away from looking like a lower-class neighborhood in Philly. The driver went to call the apartment owner and told me to stay in the car while he made the connection. My head was on a swivel, but I was slightly distracted by a woman on the sidewalk who looked like she was doing the greatest job of roasting peanuts. Before I could convince myself to buy a bag of peanuts, the apartment owner came out and introduced himself as Mr. Diop, and we headed for the apartment building. I did see a picture on a wall of Cheikh Anta Diop during my ride over, but I was not sure if this Mr. Diop had any relation to the great historian and physicist. I later learned that many people have the last name Diop in Dakar.

Mr. Diop was not wearing designer clothing, but it was obvious by his African attire that he did not live in the area and he was at least somewhat well off. The driver told me that the price of the ride was 10,000 CFA (West African Franc), and I immediately told him that his boss and I had agreed on one Euro. At that time, 10,000 CFA was about 17 American dollars, so we were on two completely different pages. He told me that the Euro was for the phone call and I was to pay him for the ride. I realized that I had gotten hustled, and now I had to contemplate whether this was worth arguing over.

I was out of cash, so the apartment owner said he would provide the money if I paid him back. I wanted to argue the charge, but I did not want to cause a scene, and I felt that I needed to be respectful in the country where I was a guest. Once we were ready to go up to the room, the driver said he wanted to go up and see it also. He had one of those distrustful faces that you use when you are telling your mom a lie. At that point, I was forced to snap out of tourist mode and I told him that he had better not put one foot on those stairs. The apartment owner told the man to go on his way, because I obviously was not here for games. I'm not sure what he was going to do if he found out where I was sleeping, but I knew it was not going to be anything positive.

After the taxi fiasco was over, I made it up to the room and it looked the same as the pictures that I saw online. Mr. Diop explained the neighborhood to me and told me about what restaurants were around, and then went on his way. After he left, the wi-fi connection suddenly went out, and when I called him back, he said he would have it fixed. An hour went by, and I couldn't leave because I did not know what was around me without any wi-fi. The room was a great deal, but I had to make the quick decision to leave it, because my stay in Dakar would pointless without any wi-fi (the Airbnb policy states that you have to leave by a certain amount of time in order to receive a refund). I used my data to find a hotel with working wi-fi that was affordable. I found something close to the dock that seemed to be in a somewhat touristy section, with easier access to landmarks.

One interesting thing about my first apartment was that even though it appeared to be in a lower-class neighborhood, it looked as if everyone owned their own stores, and their morale was generally positive. I'd never been to that city before, and it was not a touristy area, but I never feared for my safety at all. But without wi-fi, it would be impossible to walk around aimlessly trying to map out the city. Even as an adventurer, trying to get around a city that I was not familiar with while not even speaking the language was a little too extreme for me.

I collected my belongings and found a taxi to take me to the hotel, telling myself I would figure things out once I made it to my new room. When we arrived, I noticed that the neighborhood was more city-like than the apartment where I had planned to stay. There were a good number of people hanging around outside, and it appeared that this was a residential section, even though it was so close to the docks. The room was not the best, and it was loud outside, but at least the wi-fi was decent and I had a sense of my location. I did not want to spend the rest of the night in the hotel, so I found a nice restaurant at the Radisson Blu hotel.

When I'd researched the prices before traveling to Dakar, I'd seen that the Radisson Blu was about 300 US dollars for a night's stay. When I pulled up the front gate, I began to realize why it cost so much. The front parking terrace there is wide open, and its grand entrance is elegant, like a picture-book hotel. The security was solid—I had to show my passport and go through a metal detector to get inside. Once I made it down to the restaurant area, I thought I was walking into one of my dreams, because the view of the water outside was so fascinating. Someone really took their time planning the bar and pool setup, because it allowed you to look at the ocean while you enjoyed your meal or had a drink with friends. When I walked outside, there was a band playing, and I did not even care much about food at that point, because the ambience was so astonishing.

After the band finished playing, I went to see what the restaurant had to offer by way of fine dining. The decor was exceptional, and I was glad that it was not crowded, so I would be comfortable during my meal. The service was of high quality, and they were careful to explain all the options that I had for dinner. I have honestly never had a better meal experience anywhere in the world than in this hotel. I was not going to pay $300 for a room, but I did not mind paying for the wonderful meals they were offering. All of the staff spoke excellent English, and they were happy that a young, Black American had made it over to visit their country. I did not want to get too comfortable, however, because I knew the type of room I was headed back to was basically the opposite of the Radisson Blu.

After a long night of uncomfortable sleep, I got up early to watch the sunrise from the deck in my room. That day, I made the choice to move to a well-known hotel chain by the water, with the hopes of getting a better night of sleep. The hotel was brighter, cleaner, and had breakfast, which was all I needed to feel comfortable. Another plus was that the hotel was in a busy marketplace neighborhood even closer to the docks. I planned to stay at the hotel for a few days and pick a day to walk to the ferry, so I could go to the Ile de Goree and learn more about the history of Senegal. For my first full day, I made the decision to take a trip to the mall area near the Radisson Blu.

Senegal was the first time I felt like a seasoned vet when it came to bartering cab fares. Whenever I negotiated a cab fare, I did my best impression of a car salesman negotiating a price. After a while, it became a game to me and I saw it as a way to connect with the taxi drivers. Once the drivers realize that you are capable of negotiating, they tell you to just get in the car and then you both can come up with a price later. This time, though, I told the driver my price from the start when I went to the mall, and I was not going to budge. He wanted the fare for the ride up and also wanted to guarantee for the fare back to the hotel. I learned from my trip from the airport that I had to be solid on my price and make everything clear up front.

The mall was a lot like the one I saw in Kenya, with a modern look and plenty of shops catering to tourists. I was slightly disappointed that the food court choices were similar to the selections you might find in the States. One thing that did catch my eye was the African clothing they had for men, along with some sort of slippers to match. The clothes ranged from simple and relaxed to bold and colorful ones with plenty of pizzazz. I did not want to buy on impulse, so I decided to wait until I saw all the shops in the area. As I drove back to the hotel, I got to see more of the recreational opportunities along the coast and the development that Dakar was going through. A major eye catcher was a long strip of workout stations in front of the water. There was a set of old stations and then a long set of new workout stations that were free for anybody looking to workout. I instantly thought how amazing it would be if each big city in America had a long strip of weight-lifting stations for people to work out at their leisure.

I finally made it back to the hotel and, of course, the driver gave me the rundown of how he stayed with me during the whole trip, and he deserved more money. After much back and forth between French and English, I was saved by the guards at the hotel, shaming the man and saying that he shouldn't be pressing me in this manner. I can usually tell when the taxi drivers believe that they are offering a good price, because the sentences are usually short and there's no budge at all. Once I hear the bargaining and patronizing talk, I sense that they smell a couple of extra bucks they can put in their pocket.

I walked around the neighborhood for a while to see what was in the area, along with the possible places I would have to walk through when I went to the ferry for the Ile de Goree. The supermarket had the same things that you might find in America, along with the same layout. This was an unpredictable occurrence for me, because even Europe usually has a different market layout than the US. As I walked through the streets, I could see that some people thought I was a local, but many caught on that I was a tourist and quickly tried to sell me on their clothes or crafts. As an adventurer, it was easy to take a strong liking to the area because it was surrounded by hotels, but it did not feel like a tourist-heavy section.

I was glad I had made the quick decision to change my sleeping arrangements, but I still had the dilemma of deciding where I would stay for the remaining nine days. I had only chosen to stay ten days in Senegal because the Airbnb apartment was so cheap, but now that I was depending on hotels, it was going to be much more expensive. I still had one more day remaining at the hotel by the docks, so I was going to use the next day to walk to Ile de Goree ferry and spend the whole day exploring there. The positive aspect of the dilemma was that instead of only living in that one area with the apartment, I now was comfortable enough and actually had the opportunity to look for multiple places to stay in the city. Mr. Diop was fine with me changing my bedding arrangements, but I still had to return the key and the 10,000 CFA that he gave me for the taxi.

Through social media pictures and stories, I had heard that there was much learn on the Ile De Goree, so I arose the next morning on a mission, headed for the ferry. I did not know exactly where the ferry was, but I had an idea to walk along the dock and figured that I would just happen to run into it. As soon as I started my walk in the morning, I was greeted by a young guy (maybe the same age as me) and he offered to show me how to get to the ferry. Of course, I declined and acted too proud, figuring it was a hustle, but he was determined to show me the way. The Google Maps trail that I loaded gave me confidence that I would be able to get there, but I was wrong, and I really did need his help. While we walked through a long strip of street stores, the gentleman explained his connections with clothes and all the places he could help me find in the city. I usually tune these conversations out in my head when I travel (especially when alone), because I cannot say I was really focused on any clothes or clubs. My only focus at the time was Ile de Goree and how difficult the process to get there would be.

Once we got in line, I realized that his goal was to help someone to the ferry with the hopes of them paying his way as well. Unfortunately, there were no ATMs, and I only had enough to pay for my own fare, so he walked off and I concluded that I would not see that brother again. After a small wait, I set off for the island on a boat crowded full of tourists. I did not manage to get a good seat on the boat, so I was stuck on the inside trying to get a decent view of the water during the short ride. An elderly lady sitting across from me could tell that I was a tourist and casually insisted that I needed to stop by her crafts shop when I got to the island. I truly only came for history lesson, and buying crafts was not something I was looking forward to at all. To be transparent, I had done minimal research on the island, so I still had no idea what to expect once I got there. I knew there was a history of slave trading on the island, but I was not sure what it had transitioned to over the years.

The arrival at the Ile de Goree was amazing, but also strange for me. The island was beautiful, but I somehow still felt the tangible oppression of slavery as we pulled up to the dock. Since I knew the history of the island, being able to see it for myself definitely felt awkward, considering that my ancestors possibly had to take a similar ride, but not for a vacation. Near the stores, there was a gentleman gathering people, telling us that we had to pay a tax. I did not want to be disrespectful to the island's rules, but when it comes to being a tourist, I'm never sure who's lying when I have to spend money. Long story short, I weaseled my way out of the tax and walked a different trail to the House of Slaves.

The small island had a sandy layout of brightly colored houses that made me feel like I could walk in and immediately be welcomed as family. I walked around the neighborhood a little and smelled fresh bread being baked and some fresh roses outside the houses. The tour at the House of Slaves did not start until two in the afternoon, so I had time to walk through the island and study the small village nearby. While walking through the back trails of the island, I stumbled on a small market where several women were selling clothes and accessories. I really planned to only be there for a few minutes and grab some gifts for my family, but this somehow turned into a quest for a perfect bargain.

While I was killing time at the small marketplace, I was waved at by a craftswoman in the middle of the island. At first it was the usual "look for a quick sell to an American" routine, but the more pieces I looked at, the more we became like family. All the bracelets, crafts, and necklaces were creative and very unique. It's amazing how these pieces are handcrafted throughout the day, but I still wondered how the craftswomen let them sell for so little. It's possible that it's naturally easy for them to make these crafts, due to their work ethic, and my American mind is so used to having some mega manufacturer make things for me. Anyway, the clothes sell for reasonable prices, and I decided that I really would need to purchase something for myself and some pieces for my family. I did not have much cash on hand, so I was not sure how much I could buy, but she insisted that she would give me a great deal for whatever I could pay.

I quickly learned that this is a highly competitive market, and there aren't many rules when it comes to stealing buyers. Many other craftswomen interrupted my shopping to let me know that their shop was on the other side of the wall and the products were most likely higher quality. This is sort of a culture shock for me, since I'm used to being followed around a store because I'm not buying fast enough. As I continued to look at the clothes, the first craftswoman told me her story about how she did not get many customers and she needed the money to feed her kids. She explained that she worked all day and barely got to see her kids, but this market was the best opportunity for her to make money. I could see it in her face and hear it in her voice that this was not some hustle, so I had no problem looking for an ATM to buy a little more than I intended.

Of course, on an island in Africa, you are really taking a huge gamble depending on money from an ATM. I tried to get money from the island ATM, but my bank card and the machine seemed to be on two different pages. I felt bad because I really wanted to help her, but things were looking bleak. I picked out a few things and told her I would come back once I checked out the other side of the market where they had some dashikis. I paid them the rest of the currency I had left in my book bag, because, from the dashikis to the accessories, everything they had was a Pan-Africanist dream. I worked out a deal where everybody at the market could get a share of my sales and be able to log a purchase. After the long conversation with the first craftswoman, she was not even worried about the revenue anymore. She told me, "You're my brother," and said I could take whatever accessories and give whatever I had. An idea to take fifteen minutes for shopping turned into an hour and a half ordeal, but it was well worth it.

It was finally time to go to the House of Slaves to learn more about the slave trade that happened in Senegal. I walked back towards the building where the exhibit was held, and along the way I passed another elderly lady who was selling crafts. She was also selling the sticks that people chew to clean their teeth. I bought one, and it can probably be classified as an impulse buy, in order to fit in with the others, but I felt like it was a necessity at the time. It turned out to be a smart purchase because I was able to use the bathroom at the house of the lady who sold me the sticks. The house did not necessarily have a complete roof, and the bathroom was just a hole in the ground that led to the surrounding water. I'm pretty sure this was common throughout the island, because the way of life there was very old school, without much electricity or technology. The necessities that I was used to in the States, or even on the Dakar mainland, were nowhere in sight on this island. The chickens and goats weren't caged at all, and they appeared to roam freely on the families' properties

The House of Slaves was surreal, because the rooms where they had kept the slaves were very small, and I'm sure they had had them stacked on top of each other. I went inside one of the rooms and looked out through the tiny barred windows, and I felt one of the most hopeless feelings you can have. After a small tour through the house, a gentleman gave a presentation about the history of the site and the aftermath of everything. The gentleman was speaking in French, but I was able to understand most of the speech and learn about the conditions that the slaves had been held in. The back of the house has a great view of the water from down below and from the deck on the second floor of the house.

Unfortunately, the bottom view is called the "Door of No Return," because once the slaves left through that door and got on a boat, that would usually be their last view of Senegal, or even worse, Africa.

I was satisfied with my trip to the island, as the exhibit was very informative, so I prepared to head back to the mainland. Somehow, I did not factor in the idea that other people would be headed back to the mainland at the same time, and the line turned out to be at least a two-hour wait. There were a few restaurants in the area, so it made sense to kill time by enjoying the view of the island over a meal. I had been making a strong effort to add more fish to my diet, and there was no better place to continue that initiative than on an African island. I chose a John Dory fish platter with a bissap drink to match, and my evening was set. The John Dory platter consisted of a delicious baked fish fillet with rice and a cream sauce. The bissap drink is made from hibiscus flowers, and the taste is simply delectable. I could imagine that the non-alcoholic bissap drink would cost around eight US dollars, but the concoction was very cheap in Senegal.

The line did not budge at all, and it appeared that I still had a two-hour wait from the end of the line. I really had no choice at this point, because it was getting dark and the temperature was dropping rapidly. The first hour was pretty boring, and the breeze that had been so wonderful during the hot afternoon had turned into a cold, violent wind that was sure to make me sick. All of a sudden, a drum started beating in the front of the line, and people started to sing lightly. After about twenty minutes, that soft African singing turned into a loud concert and everybody started dancing. The sight of tourists and locals singing and dancing together in line to this drum was an unforgettable experience. The use of a drum and the combined voices turned a cold and tiring atmosphere into a party-like environment.

After a cold boat ride back to the mainland, I was determined to get back to my room to put on the proper clothing for a brisk night by the water. I still had to return the keys and money to Mr. Diop, but I also met someone from France, who invited me to hang out with her friend who lived in Dakar. I'm not the nightlife type of guy in any sense, but I was looking forward to seeing how they party in Africa. I got changed and hailed a cab to head back to the apartment where I had first stayed. Mr. Diop gave me the name and number of somebody I could give the keys and money to, but it was slightly difficult to find the building at night. The neighborhoods really reminded me of some parts of Philly, only with sanded sidewalks and fewer fast food restaurants.

We zipped through the night, turning down narrow driveways and skidding on dusty roads. After the eventful ride, the taxi arrived at the apartment, and the driver asked a young guy from the neighborhood for help on how to find the gentleman Mr. Diop had told me about. It turned out that the gentleman was in a small corner store. The encounter ran smoothly, and I was able to close that chapter of my trip. The neighborhood may have been lower class, but even during the night time, I never felt any dangerous vibes. I do not say that to mean I was surprised, but to show that I felt safe in a random draw of Dakar's neighborhoods.

The area where I was to meet my friends was towards the airport and the photos online made it look like a pretty high class place, so I was not worried about any problems. The venue was basically a bar around a pool, but it was decorated well. The evening was enjoyable until it got really cold out. After leaving the small party, we went searching for a nice local club to get an idea of Dakar's nightlife. Once we arrived at the strip, I was surprised by how much the busy avenue looked like a club scene in Atlanta. I was all the way in Africa, but it looked like we were somewhere I had been in the deep south. We entered one club, and the vibe inside was more like a club I might find at home in Philly. It had plenty of strobe lights, but there was not a lot of dancing. Many people just staring you in the face with a blank look, and consequently were way too cool to seem like they were having fun. We checked out a few more places, but it seemed like it just was not in the cards that night to go to clubs.

Of course, it would have been too simple for the night to end quietly. Things quickly became dramatic as we drove to another venue. While driving through the strip, we encountered a military security checkpoint, which was fairly normal for the area. We had already been stopped that night in another area, so we figured that it would be another basic check and we would be on our way. I gave my passport and the driver gave his information, while the two ladies handed over their information. One young lady had some form of identification that looked strange, but it had been sufficient earlier in the night, so there was no reason to worry. An officer asked her to get out of the car, and what had initially seemed like a simple checkpoint stop turned into a long plea for leniency.

I was told by the other officer that the checkpoints are necessary because there are dangerous criminals who try to slip in and out of different countries while they're on the run. So it's important to have identification with you when traveling in certain parts of Africa, and you also need to make sure that your hotel or apartment owner has your information or identification somewhere, so they can confirm it if you run into problems. The checkpoints were very random, like police DUI checkpoints. I knew this because we had not even been trying to access a special event or an exclusive area. I honestly figured that they would let us go after about fifteen minutes, because the young lady had a very respectable job in the city and she did not have the aura of a criminal.

An hour later, we were still trying to see how we could get around this problem, having given up the idea that we could still find a place to go after this fiasco. The officer finally yielded and implied the young lady was OK to go, but that he wanted her number. I couldn't quite make out the French they were speaking, but I'm sure that that had been his motive from the beginning of the checkpoint stop. I'm not sure how long the ordeal lasted, but it was enough to put me in my slumber zone, and my eyes were getting extremely heavy. We bargained for a taxi to take us back to our respective hotels, and I looked forward to packing my bags and going to Ngor Island the next day. After he slammed into almost every speed bump possible, I started to suspect that the driver was either drunk or as sleepy as I was. The drive back to my hotel was about a half hour, and this driver was having mini car crashes with the bumps in the ground. By God's grace, I made it back to my room and rested after an eventful day.

I woke up the next morning with a desire to walk around the neighborhood a little before it was time to leave the hotel. I was surprised to find the same man that walked me to the Goree ferry was waiting for me at the hotel gate. He said that he wanted to take me to his father's shop at Marché Sandaga, where I could buy some dashikis and some of the Moroccan slides I had seen earlier in the week. I felt comfortable because I could discern that he was honest enough to walk with and was probably just trying to make a sale.

The walk to the market was about a mile and a half across town, and it gave me the chance to view the everyday life in Dakar. The area was sprinkled with mom and pop stores mixed in with well-known clothing stores on the same street. The closer we got to the Sandaga market, the poorer the condition of the houses and stores became.

We arrived at the store and the gentleman's father introduced himself as Mr. Boubacar and greeted me in Wolof, the national language of Senegal. He continued the conversation in Wolof, and after a couple of sentences he realized that I was not from Senegal. It actually made me feel good and welcome that somebody thought I was from the country and I could fit in. He spoke French and English well, so it was very easy to communicate with him. His store was one among hundreds in the area, but it was clean and well-structured in order to entice potential buyers. I had an idea of the pieces that I wanted to buy, but with so many choices of fabrics and colors, I struggled to make decisions. He sent me to one room and the walls had several dashikis, and when I looked up, there was almost every African pattern ever made. Mr Boubacar said that he had a bigger factory store down the street, and he could show me even more fabrics and designs at that location.

The factory store looked like it could be an old school building, but all the floors had fabrics and machines wall to wall, so there were only small aisles that you could walk through to get around. I went to his store on the second floor and spent even more time marveling at all of the precious fabrics that I could choose from. I picked a few fabrics so I could have some shirts custom made and I also selected some of the already made dashikis. Based on his willingness to let me choose before giving a price, I knew the negotiation process would be interesting but fun. Of course I wanted a great deal, but I also did not want to act like I was broke. I had previously bought much less desired pieces from European stores that did not care if I made a purchase or not. So I was torn: I was thankful for being appreciated, but also trying not to get hustled as an American. After acting like I was making a tough decision, I threw a number out, then he frowned and came back with another number. After a few more number exchanges, Mr. Boubacar threw the fabric down in a slight tantrum, which caught me by surprise, but I knew it was an act to get me to go along with his price. I chuckled on the inside and kept a straight face as we continued the negotiations. We agreed on a temporary number, but we both knew that when I came back in a couple days for the custom pieces, I would buy more. I told him I would return for the pieces and pay for them when I got back from Ngor Island, and we could then start a second round of negotiations.

CHAPTER 13

Ngor Island

I began to appreciate every aspect of Senegal as I anticipated each new experience. The transition between my lodging in the different areas of Dakar allowed me to get a better understanding of the city overall. The small setback of having to leave the first apartment because of no wi-fi turned out to be a blessing because of how it had allowed me to search for different hotels. I saw an Airbnb listing on Ngor Island that was rather cheap, not to mention that the house looked nice and it was also a chance to stay on an island. The ferry for the island was not far from where I had gone the night before to see the nightlife. My previous hotel was in South Dakar, and Ngor Island sits on the north edge of the city, so I had to play hardball to get a decent price for the long taxi ride. My French at the time was very basic and limited at best, but it's difficult in the best of times to pronounce Ile de Ngor. The driver did not quite know how to get there, and we got lost a few times on the way, so I was sure that there would be a request for more money when we arrived.

I had been advised that the vibe on Ngor Island is totally different from what you might find closer to the tourist sections in South Dakar. That information was confirmed when I arrived, as I immediately felt a Bob Marley, Rastafarian ambience at the Ngor

Island dock. The owner of the apartment told me to look for a Monsieur Salin, who owned a ferry boat, and he would give me a ride to the island. After a phone call, Mr. Salin came over to walk me towards the beach so I could get settled in the apartment where I was staying for the next few days. Once I got to the sand, it was clear that hanging by the beach was a way of life for some of the locals. Mr Salin's boat business looked to be a smooth and easy one for somebody in their late thirties. He and his employees hung by the water and enjoyed the day while they waited for tourists who needed a lift to the island and back, collecting a per-person fee. Based on the several times I used the ferry service, the group consistently did their best to pass the day by playing games and cooking in between the various ferry trips.

The ferry ride to Ngor Island was much shorter than the Goree Island ferry, and the boats were much smaller, but it was definitely still a great experience. The first ferry ride to Ngor Island made me realize that I really was in Africa, jumping from island to island, living the dream. The boat landed smoothly on the beach at Ngor, and I tried to look as natural as possible as I hopped out of the boat with my bags. Up to this point, I could probably count on my hands the number of times I had gotten on or off a boat at a dock. As such, jumping out of a small boat into the water was slightly new to me. Since the beach does not really give you a view of what the island really looks like, I was not sure what type of building I would be staying in or what to expect in terms of island conditions.

Mr. Salin and I were met by a young lady who took us up to the apartment and said she could answer any questions that I had about the house. While transitioning from the sand to the cement walkway, we passed four mom-and-pop grill restaurants that were right next to the water, and the smell coming from them was fresh and satisfying. I hadn't eaten before my long morning journey to the island, so my attention span was short while walking through the house. I was not aware that the booking came with two housekeepers who would help whenever they were able to throughout the day. The entrance was right off of the island's premier walkway, and the house had a cement fort around it and a locking door. The house was designed well, and it was equipped with a television, wi-fi, and a well-equipped kitchen. There were two rooms upstairs, along with a deck that looked out onto the water, which would serve as a great place to eat my breakfast.

The housekeeper named Adja could see that I was hungry, and she said she would walk me back to the restaurants to introduce me to one of the owners. Chez Aminta, the restaurant to which she took me, was a stand about the size of a vendor's box. It wouldn't have looked out of place at a food truck market event in the States. The grill, along with the marinades and sauces, were all laid out for me to see, and I was even able to watch someone bring in the latest fish catch while sitting at my table. All the food was made to order, and the smell of the marinated chicken on the grill made me even hungrier while I waited. Ms. Aminta offers several local non-alcoholic drinks that you can enjoy while waiting. I made a safe decision to go with the bissap drink that I had ordered when I was on Ile de Goree. It became clear that this drink has a consistently great taste, and that you can find it almost anywhere in the country of Senegal for a reasonable price.

The chicken and rice platter was served with a special green sauce, vinaigrette salad, and French fries. Based on the smell of the food alone, I could tell every ingredient was fresh. The food was nourishing, but being able to enjoy my meal and sit on the sand while the water crashed at my feet was even better. On a regular day at home, I might rush through eating my food because I find it to be the best way of enjoying a great meal. In this case, the calmness of the island allowed me to enjoy my food and relax. I got to witness many colorful narrow wooden boats bringing tourists and natives back and forth from the mainland. The Ngor atmosphere is calm, but there is still steady business going on and a great deal of harmony between the natives. One thing I did notice was that out of the four restaurants on the beachfront of Ngor Island, they all seem to cook the same thing, but they utilize some sort of teamwork. Throughout my visits to Chez Aminta, I never got the sense that anybody was in competition, and they helped each other if one place was lacking something. I thanked Ms. Aminta and put together my best French to tell her that her food was special. I'm sure she gets that praise a lot after someone is finished with their meal, because she wore a confident smile and thanked me.

Since I was starting to gain more confidence with my French, I took the time to get to know the housekeepers and see if there was anything more they could tell me about the island. Adja and

Moussa were both humble people and fully committed to making me feel home on the island. This was my first time being without light, electricity, and wi-fi after dark, but I saw it as a challenge that could possibly make me learn something about myself. It made sense to plan my days at the apartment with the idea that I would be on the island the majority of the time, maybe only taking a couple of trips back to the mainland to buy something at the markets. I had a kitchen now, and Adja said she would take me to the nearest supermarket to buy groceries for the house. I hadn't taken a tour of the island yet, so I had no idea if there were any stores or restaurants outside of the ones I had already seen.

While I had a strong feeling that every day would be an adventure while I was on Ngor Island, I made sure I paced myself each day, being careful not to tire myself out. Whenever I'm in a space with a kitchen, my first move is to find the nearest market, so I do not spend all of my money at the local restaurants. I also choose to cook because food preparation customs can vary depending on where you are in the world, and it's easier to get sick at a restaurant. Adja accompanied me to the nearest market, and once again, the business was just like any supermarket that you would find in America. Even still, I was shocked at how many non-Africans I saw shopping at the market. Some spoke French and others English, but it was obvious that Europeans made up a great portion of the demographics in this area.

I did not have all the spices and ingredients that I usually use when I cook, but I made a simple chicken platter, and it was obvious that Adja was not impressed by my American cuisine. She told me that she would cook an African dish called Yassa Poulet the next day, and that I would be sure to like it. Adja was more than willing to give me a tour of the island and show me the places I could go during my stay at the house. Goree was a rather easy place to walk around with just flip flops on, but Adja assured me that Ngor was far more rocky with less sand, so sneakers would be necessary for some of the paths.

The main walkway gives the illusion that the island is a small village with only a small path for walking in between the properties. However, when we walked farther beyond the house I was staying, the path opened up, and there were a few more houses. The back of the island has open land with big boulders where the water crashes on the beach. There are too many boulders for a beach setting, but the blue water crashing on the black rocks creates a great place for relaxation and reflection. After witnessing the many natural precious points of the area, it was easy to understand why most of the people around the island were so carefree.

The more I walked around the island, the more the artistry of the properties increased, and it was clear that art was a point of pride on this specific island. Aside from the paintwork on the sides of the houses, many crafts sat outside of the different properties. Many inhabitants devote their day to producing crafts and displaying them for sale while they work. I had the pleasure of meeting a couple of the artists, who continued the Rastafarian theme that was present throughout the island. The highest point of Ngor Island is at the very back of the 325 square foot piece of land, where I could watch surfers and waves flow below. Some of the local artists even took time to construct cement benches speckled with decorative glass patterns. You could easily spend hours sitting at those benches looking out at the water. Even on the small island of Ngor, each neighborhood had a different theme and way of life.

Ngor Island does not appear to be large in size at all, but its design is so well structured that the houses and various buildings fit together perfectly. Across from my apartment on the far side of the island, the properties were closer together and slightly more upscale. Adja took me to the apartment owner's house, with the hopes of introducing me, but he was not home at the time. The house had a security gate on the front, but the large, modern home (which would not have been out of place in Los Angeles) gave me the idea that he might have a good amount of money. He may have had the best house on the island, but there were a few other properties that had much more land. I saw a couple of spaces that were either vacant or the house was dilapidated, which gave me some personal real estate ideas for the future. This side of the island emptied into another small beach that had one restaurant and a more intimate vibe compared to the beach where I first arrived.

On the walk back to the apartment, I noticed that there was a military base in the direct center of the island. My height allowed me to see over the walls as I walked by. There was not much equipment visible, but there did seem to be hundreds of soldiers present at the base. Throughout my time on the island, I could see troops jogging through the different parts of the island for cardio and training. Overall, I was impressed with the island because of how the small space was utilized, and the fact that even though it's a tourist attraction, they were still able to keep it like a small town. Even with a military base and multiple houses taking up a lot of space, the island also has a well-decorated school that looks like it is newly built.

While I was back at the apartment, it was normal for Moussa and Adja to sit in the living room with me while I watched TV. The house was split up vertically into three different apartments, but the two of them still felt comfortable enough to hang around with me. There was not much on television that I cared to watch, but Moussa liked watching the local soccer matches, and Adja took an interest in the Black American "reality" shows that had been translated into French. Adja was maybe twenty-three or twenty-four, but she seemed to be very intelligent and far from lazy. Every day she would bring her cosmetic doll and work on different hairstyles while she was passing time throughout the day. She told me that it was her goal to someday own a hair salon in New York and live the American Dream. I had my opinions about the so-called "American Dream," but I did not feel like it was my place to say anything that might discourage her.

I did notice that Adja paid close attention to the Black "reality" shows where there is constant bickering, poor decisions, and a lot of fighting, and I was immediately embarrassed. Outside of sports and entertainment, I did not see many instances where people in Africa might be able to see the real, everyday life of Black Americans. I acknowledge that we're in trouble if these "reality" shows are all they get to see in Africa. I tried my best to explain that a lot of what she saw on television was possibly scripted. and even still only a small fraction of Black Americans. At the end of the day, Adja is only one person, but I'm sure there are tons of other girls watching these shows trying to mimic the nonsense in hopes of making it on TV one day as well.

My diet was changing rapidly from being away from America for so long, and I began to add new recipes weekly. Adja showed me how to make Yassa Chicken and Yassa Fish with the ingredients I got from the store and a few of her own spices. I'd never had the idea of making a mustard-based sauce in a pan with vegetables, but the taste was incredible, and there was zero chance for leftovers. The flavors were truly Senegalese, and the directions were simple-but-detailed with the spices that they used. My goal was to add more Senegalese dishes to my repertoire during my time there, with the hopes of replacing my go-to dishes of chicken alfredo and beef and broccoli.

I would've stayed at Ngor Island longer, but the house was booked for the remainder of my trip. I glanced at local hotel prices on the mainland, hoping the Radisson Blu Hotel was a bit cheaper than before. As it turned out, the hotel price per night was significantly lower, so I packed my bags and headed back to the mainland to finish out my trip in brief luxury. But before I did that, I did have to return to Marché Sandaga to retrieve the dashikis that I'd bought before I left for Ngor Island. Before I returned to the mainland, Adja offered to go to the market area with me to help shop for clothes. I figured that I might get a better price on dashikis if I had someone who spoke the language to help me avoid paying too much. She told me about a couple of her friends' stores that we could also visit for a deal on clothes. After one last boat ride with Mr. Salin, I said goodbye to Ngor Island, with strong desires to return in the future.

The Radisson Blu was luxurious, but somehow there was an open vent that allowed mosquitoes to buzz by my ear while I tried to sleep. I was initially frustrated, because I'd paid a lot of money for luxury, but the stay was getting ruined by mosquitoes. My annoyance quickly evolved into fear, since this was at the height of the Zika Virus epidemic, and I was in Africa, about to get bitten by multiple mosquitoes. The staff did what they could to get rid of the problem, but I tried to solve it on my own by killing as many as I could before asking for help. I didn't see any more after the first housekeeping rounds.

The Radisson was in a great area, located by a long commercial strip that its guests could explore if they wanted to. I had already been to the mall, so I walked down even further to the long strip of workout stations that I'd seen earlier. I got in a few workouts, and even though there were tons of different stations, almost all of them were being used. After my workout, I went farther down the coastal strip, where I saw a raw coconut stand and decided this would be a great time to cross that experience off of my bucket list. It may seem rather simple for most, but there aren't many things you can get from a tree in Philly, so this was a privilege. After the vendor took his machete and took a few hacks at the coconut, I sat down and watched a pickup soccer game while I tried fresh coconut water for the first time.

The next day I headed to Marché Sandaga, with the hopes of walking away with a deal that Mr. Boubacar and I could both be satisfied with. After meeting Adja at the market area, she showed me different stores where the prices for dashiki sets were far below what I had seen before. After making a few purchases, we went over to Mr. Boubacar's store to play the African version of *Let's Make a Deal*. Once I arrived at the store, Mr Boubacar was shocked that I had somebody that could speak Wolof. They had a Wolof conversation and he was quick to tell me about the difference in their last names and how his was better. He brought out the pieces that I had ordered and threw a number out to see if I would go along with it. I asked Adja about the number and she instantly told me that I should be getting more for what I was paying.

After picking out a few more pieces, our negotiations finally found a compromise, and I thanked Adja and Mr Boubacar for their help. The help that they gave me made me feel like I was more than just a random tourist passing through. The transaction was genuine and left the door open for the future. I knew I'd be back in Dakar in the near future, so I did not act like I'd be too distant.

I knew my vacation would end once I got back to Toulouse, France, so I did my best to enjoy those last days at the Radisson Blu hotel. The sea bass dinner I had at the Radisson was by the far the best I have ever had. The fish was plated with Pomme Anna (layered potatoes) and a sweet potato sauce that I could have never imagined was possible to create. It, along with Pomme Anna, is something that appears to be difficult to organize and prepare, but the heavenly taste makes it worth it. The meal was so good that I had to restrain myself from ordering the same thing right after I finished. I'm glad that this was not one of those robot waiter restaurants, because the only thing that stopped me from a second order was the fact that I was too embarrassed for someone to know I was that greedy. I substituted that second helping with a calm night by the pool, looking out at the ocean wondering when I would return to Dakar and what African country and city would I see next.

After a wonderful three days at the Radisson Blu Hotel, I took a taxi to the Leopold Sédar Senghor International Airport to prepare for my return back to Toulouse. I began to miss Senegal before I had even left the country. During my taxi ride, I noticed a large military truck riding in front of us with a French flag on the back. I had an idea that France had some dealings in Senegal, but I was not sure to what extent. I asked the taxi driver to explain further, and his brief explanation was along the lines of France having an air force base in the country. I was not sure if an air force base was the extent of France's dealings in Senegal, but it was quite interesting to be in a country and see a foreign country with their military trucks present. I made my flight on time and got ready to return to the cold days of February in France.

CHAPTER 14

Tour de France

When I landed back in Toulouse, I did not know if my new friend Chadi was going to come through for me with a comfortable place to rent. Coach Aboudou met me at the airport and drove me to a neighborhood in Toulouse that I had never seen before, called Arenes. We had to go through some apartment insurance paperwork and then went to the apartment complex where I would possibly be staying. Since the apartment building was right next to the tram and not far from a metro station, traveling around Toulouse was not going to be difficult. The building was traditionally for college students in the area, but Chadi was able to pull some strings so I could find a comfortable space. The room was newly designed and had a desk, a flat-screen television, and a spacious bathroom. I was very thankful to God for my international friends and their diligence to make sure I had a place to stay in France.

Now that I was back in France and my vacation was over, it was imperative that I get back in top physical shape in time for any basketball tryouts coming up. I went back to the basketball gym where I had been working out before and renewed my membership for another month. I noticed that there was a fitness center next to the gym that had just opened, and everybody told me that the machines were state of the art. Fitness centers are usually expensive in France, for whatever reason, but nothing would be more convenient than being able to lift weights and then walk next door to shoot around and run drills. The monthly price was rather high, but there was no initiation fee, and two months was a great deal if I was going to be working out five days a week.

The workout space was better than any fitness center I've ever seen, and since the location was far off from the city, the gym was never crowded. The gym staff was very welcoming and also appeared to be a little shocked that I was a non-fluent French speaker from America. Americans are commonly found in the bigger cities like Paris, but rarely found in the smaller cities like Toulouse. At this point, I was visiting a new place almost every week, so I was comfortable with people giving a me a tour and explaining directions in French. I was also amazed at how interested people were in my story about being from the United States and finding my way to a distant town in France. Since the gym was just starting out and I consistently attended throughout the week, it did not take long for me to become acquainted with all of the staff and practice my French from time to time.

During my basketball workouts on the court with Coach Aboudou, a teenager walked up and started cheering me on and encouraging me to keep going, as he could see I was wearing down. I thought it was bizarre, because that's never happened to me in the States, and I'd never had a conversation with this kid before. After the workout, he introduced himself as Phu and explained his desire to improve his basketball game so that he could find a local youth team to play for. He said that he was originally from the Philippines and explained the difficulty of trying to find a team, since he did not have French citizenship. He was certain that working on his basketball game with me after school would help his chances; I agreed and decided that it was time to change my workout routine anyway.

After practicing with Phu for a couple weeks, I began to realize that Phu was basically me at seventeen. We both had the same work ethic, goals, and a few basketball-related mechanical errors that had to be corrected. Being able to see him go after his dream helped fuel my own aspirations, I knew I couldn't show any doubt or appear weak during the workouts, because it may have been detrimental to his work ethic. After a few setbacks and disappointments, Phu eventually found a team, and I was glad I could be a small help in his development. By witnessing the process of him achieve only the first part of his dream, I realized that I needed to appreciate my challenge, and that I would eventually achieve my goal of finding a great basketball club to play for.

Even though I've been fortunate to travel to many wonderful places, my Philadelphia background has given me the knowledge, experience, and comfort of taking public transportation any place that I go. Toulouse's suburbs aren't the easiest places to get to in terms of public transportation, because many places are being developed, and the bus routes have not been updated yet. I would take two buses to get to the gym, and after reaching the end of the line for the bus in the area of Sept Derniers, I would still have to walk another ten minutes in the often muddy grass to get to the gym. The two metro lines inside the city were well placed, and the tram lines, along with the buses, made most of the city rather easy to get to. My experiences with slow Septa service in Philadelphia made me appreciate the rapid transit of the metro in Toulouse. Trains usually ran every three or four minutes, and buses usually ran every ten minutes during the day.

I was very consistent with going to the gym daily, but I knew it would likely take more initiative to find a team and make connections for the future. I already made a few French connections over time, but I felt like I needed to go talk to some teams myself while I was in the country. I noticed that the city of Limoges was not too far from Toulouse, and a bus ride was rather inexpensive for a day trip. Limoges had a top division team, and I thought it was a great idea to go to a game and see what the way of life was like in the city. I was also beginning to enjoy seeing different French cities, and the thought of possibly finding a city to settle in later on in life when I'm done playing basketball. I had been to Paris and some cities in the south of France, but I had never been to any cities closer to central France. Visiting the city of Limoges would give me a different view of the country.

Since Limoges is about three hours from Toulouse, my lack of comfort in a bus seat was not too extensive, and there was no way I could imagine the buses being as packed as my trips to Barcelona, so that also helped. I decided to take an early bus ride to Limoges and then take a late bus back to Toulouse after the game, in order to avoid the hassle of the hotel booking process and packing bags.

Another reason that I had an interest in Limoges was that one of their former players was the late, great Michael Brooks, who was also from Philadelphia. As a Philadelphian who had a passion to play and coach basketball, Michael Brooks' story inspired me a great deal, and I thought it would be great if I could see and possibly play in the city that he had graced.

The central transportation station of Gare de Limoges-Bénédictins in Limoges looks just like one of those monstrous pieces of art that you would see in your middle school social studies class. The vibe in Limoges was very welcoming, and the park around the station was well laid out and relaxing. I had a little difficulty understanding the public transportation, so I decided to walk through the city to the main bus hub, where I knew I could find the bus line that went to the basketball team's arena. As I walked through the city, I recognized the layout of some streets as similar to the ones in Nice. The streets were so clean, and the city shops were designed perfectly and kept up with well. In order to get to the main bus station hub, I had to walk through the main commerce section, where there was a small mall and an open concrete park surrounded by restaurants.

I happened to come to Limoges on the day of a local festival; there were many people in the streets and tons of street vendors selling food that most Americans would gladly spend their life savings on. I'm not really big on street food, but I arrived in the city during that unfortunate time where restaurants are usually not serving food while they prepare for dinner service. After floating through random streets and failing to find a good meal, I was forced to hold that thought until after the game. It would have been great to stop and enjoy the street festivities, but I was more focused on getting to the arena. I was anxious to see if there were any staff I could possibly speak with before or after the game. The bus lines at the station were extremely confusing, but I finally got my bearings straight and headed for the arena.

The European sports club system is significantly different from the system in the USA, because most of the teams in Europe consist of a club of different sports with different levels. For example, it's like your favorite basketball team also having a professional soccer team. Along with those professional teams, they manage some youth travel teams for both sports. The Limoges arena is placed in an area that looks more like a campus, and I was impressed by the obvious connection that the local fans have to the team. The Joventut arena that I had seen in Badalona was rather large, because it was initially made for the likes of an Olympic game where Michael Jordan would be playing, but the gym in Limoges was much smaller. It was possibly the size of a mid-major school's basketball gym, but Limoges CSP had a very detailed interior with very regal decorations of the team's colors.

My ticket was not that expensive, but I had a pretty nice seat in the lower rows where I could see the action. It was disappointing not be on the court playing, but it was also encouraging that I had the confidence that I could compete in the league after seeing the full match. Limoges CSP would also be an easy team to play for, since the fans were very supportive and defensive about their team and players. No English words were in any of the fan outbursts, but it was clear that the body language and faces are the same when a bad call is made. After enjoying a great game, it was obvious that I made the correct decision to visit Limoges, and there was a strong possibility that I could play for them for the future. Unfortunately, the city buses do not run after 9 PM, so I had a nice walk back to the train station in order to catch my late bus back to Toulouse.

As I settled into my new apartment in Toulouse, I was again forced to alter my appetite, because I was now without an oven. During my time in Spain, I had really cut down on sautéing with oil, beginning to cook stews and bake. Without an oven, I could only make stews, and that forced me to explore alternate ways to prepare meals. I researched many health articles and listened to lectures about eating better for more energy. My dedication to working out consistently was also a factor in searching for new ways to conserve energy. I noticed that when I stopped cooking with oil, I did not get that tired feeling in my workouts, and I had a lot of energy. I cut back on potato chips and junk food and only ate Muesli (a granola blend) and roasted unsalted peanuts. After a month, I began to shy away from anything that was in a jar or a bag and to avoid about eighty percent of the things in the supermarket.

I began to only concentrate on lamb or fish recipes in the form of a stew or soup. My first experiment was with a Caribbean fish stew recipe that I saw on Youtube. My first hurdle was going to the fish market at Marché des Carmes to actually buy the fish. I had never purchased raw fish in my life, so making the order in French was going to be difficult for several reasons. At that point in my life, I wasn't interested in raw fish, and I really wasn't impressed that the French display every fillet and chopped head in front of me. I also hadn't had much success translating the names for the fish from English to French, so I didn't really understand what fish I was looking for. The raw smell didn't help my uneasiness, but I could at least tell that everything was fresh. After a minute of concentrated gazing, I was interrupted by the clerk who was ready to slice whatever fish selection I made. I knew the French word for stew is ragout, so I told him that I wanted to cook the fish in that manner. He suggested the cabillaud, which is French for cod fish. I only heard of cod being fried and battered in the US, so I wasn't too confident in his suggestion.

Just across from the fish stand, there was a entire business dedicated to providing every cut of lamb. Chez Alexandre was a lamb lover's dream store and was owned by two amazing people. Monsieur Alexandre and his wife treated me like I was their own family from the first time I walked up to their stand. They used every opportunity they had to give me a French pronunciation lesson, always demonstrative when directing me. From lamb shanks to ground mutton, they had everything and prided themselves on knowing the proper recipe for each cut. When they had the time, they always wanted hear about my own endeavors and what my life was like in the States.

Along with fresh lamb and fish, I began to seek out fresh herbs like parsley and cilantro to add the finishing touch to my meals. The first time I prepared the tomato-based Caribbean fish stew, the first spoonful test let me know that I'd struck gold. I instantly knew that I would be cooking this dish for the rest of my life. I had never cooked with coconut milk before, but it was evident that it held all the flavors together. The Arabic lamb recipes I made turned out to be a hit also, although they were a tease for the hour I had to smell them cook in the apartment.

I did well with avoiding most unhealthy foods while in France, but the one thing I couldn't do without was fresh baked goods directly from the patisserie. The French baguettes are impossible to cut from your diet, but so are the small treats like Madeleines (really sophisticated and detailed corn muffins) and pain au raisin (raisin brioche). Americans may not understand the concept, but after a day of work in France, it's very customary to go to the bakery, get your baguette, and carry it home while you try not to eat it before your dinner. I was also beginning to feel like a true Frenchman and had the confidence to place orders at stores without being nervous. The best I could manage to do was cut back on my carbohydrate intake and refrain from keeping cash in my pocket so I couldn't buy anything at the store.

As France began to warm up after the winter, I was asked by Coach Aboudou to play in a tournament in April. The tournament was in the city of Poitiers, which had been on my radar as a possible place to stay because it had a high level basketball team.. Before coming to France, I did not know that the country had a strong African population. Most of these citizens may have come from countries that had been colonized in the past. I always knew about the connection between Ivory Coast and France, but never the likes of Madagascar, Benin, Burkina Faso, and others. Coach Aboudou was from Madagascar and had tons of family and friends in the central and south of France. The Malagasy community does a great job of organizing events and enjoying each other's company for a weekend or so. It was a great chance for me to play competitive basketball and see the culture of another community.

We only stayed in the area of Poitiers train station, but we were able to still see many great displays of historic architecture. I began to conclude that all French cities aim to keep the architecture from the past. I'm very sure that the layout and buildings in Poitiers are exactly how they were at least 200 years ago. I know the historic fabric in America is far less extensive as France, but in most American cities the goal is to change house and building structures with the times. Even new construction is far less detailed than the buildings from the 1940s and before. I took a small walk up and down the main avenue around the train station and Poitiers reminded me of small but prestigious city in the US looking to attract tourists.

When we arrived at the hotel, I was shocked that the Malagasy community was so large and connected in France. Coach Aboudou took me around to meet his family and friends, and they treated me just like I was their family, as well. Coach Aboudou had also brought in another basketball friend who was set up with a team in Paris. He introduced himself as Jimmy from the Congo, and I was glad that I was not the only person not from Madagascar at the tournament. It's always a delight to meet someone from a different country and to try to get an understanding of the atmosphere and the possibilities of traveling there. After learning about the great life of Patrice Lumumba, I've made it a goal of mine to visit the

Congo one day and learn about the people and culture. Patrice Lumumba was a independence leader from the Congo with a mission to improve the quality of life for the Congolese. After spending years fighting for the Congo's independence, he was assassinated seven months after the country was granted independence from Belgium.

As much as I was intrigued by the Congo, Jimmy and the others were interested in the story of Black Americans and what Philadelphia is like. It's a bit of a culture shock when people light up when they hear I'm from the US, because that same elation isn't present when I'm actually in the US. I've found it interesting how I do not always feel welcome in my own country, but people I meet around the world marvel at my existence as a Black American. It's a wonderful experience to meet new people in a foreign country when you are both from different areas, because the shared stories and journeys are usually unique. Jimmy and I were conversing about some of the serious problems going on in each of our cities and neighborhoods, and while the specifics were slightly different, the negative end result was the same. No matter how dire the situation may be in the Congo, I still want to visit and learn more about it.

The basketball tournament itself was perfectly organized and went smoothly, but it had a rule that only one non-Malagasy player could be on the floor at a time. Jimmy was a 6'7, low-post player, and I'm 6'5 and usually like to play on the perimeter. I honestly believe that we would have won the tournament if we had played at the same time. Whatever the case may be, rules are rules; we had to strategically set the playing time so everybody could play but also so that we had a chance at winning. Since we wound up losing in the semi-finals, the rest of the weekend was dedicated to having fun and meeting new people. The final game was held in the actual gym where the Poitiers city team plays, so it was the perfect opportunity to get a look at a potential club of mine. The arena was newly designed and spacious, and the trip fueled me to push for a spot with this club in the future.

I had only spent a minimal amount of time with the people of Madagascar for the weekend, but it was easy to tell that they're proud of their culture and that their culture is centered around family. I met many generations of my teammates' families and they really enjoyed taking the time to appreciate each other's conversation. That's not to say that this isn't something that happens in America, but to see one big group from a distant country meet up and spend the weekend together is quite amazing to me. On paper, the basis of the gathering was basketball, but it appeared to me that basketball was just the bonus of being in each other's company.

While I was there, I experienced the food and music of Madagascar and learned about the country's history. The food was a healthy mixture of vegetables, with grilled chicken or beef and white rice. I really try to refrain from eating fried foods anymore, but my friend Jimmy told me to try some of the battered and deep-fried plantains that were prepared. It was by far the best food I had in Poitiers. I only had a couple of plantains the first time, but I quickly found myself in a crowded line trying to get a second helping of them—they were delightful. The kitchen atmosphere was something that I was used to back home, with the seasoned, "Queens" of the family cooking and serving the amazing food for the flock of people.

As another sign of their national pride, the tournament's administrators held a spot in the tournament halftime for natives of Madagascar to do their tribal dances. The women were dressed in their tribal clothes and danced to music that was like a soca reggae with tribal drums. I'm quite sure that much of the dancing came from their country's culture and had originated years ago, but there was also dancing that you might see in today's hip hop scene, which was amusing to me. It was a great experience to be with people from an African country and see that our cultures do not differ much. At times, I'm not sure what the reputation of Americans is abroad, so I do not flaunt my citizenship around looking for a reaction. However, meeting many people and seeing their curiosity when they hear that I'm a Black American gave me an understanding of how many feel about our culture.

On the drive back to Toulouse, Coach Aboudou let me know that we'd be stopping in Limoges to visit his family, who were having a cookout. After a few hours, we arrived at the Limoges countryside, where a house sat on a hill with a huge backyard and nothing but grass around the property. At the cookout, there was a nice sized gathering, and a few faces that I had seen from the tournament. They made me feel at home with their hospitality. This was the most organized cookout I've seen in my life, from the food to the atmosphere. Even as we pulled up to the house, you could tell there was a positive vibe to the place, and everyone had love for each other.

When we arrived, the food was almost finished cooking and I was amazed at how everybody patiently waited to eat until there was enough grilled food for everyone. A grilled chicken and rice mixture, along with natural fruit juice, looked appetizing and well prepared for the guests. The seats at the table were reserved for the elderly members of the family, while the younger generations stood or sat on the grass and ate. The hosts stopped to announce how thankful they were for everybody coming to the cookout. After eating, all the guests took a collection for the hosting family to show their appreciation and thanked them with double cheek kisses before they left. After a short post-meal treat of fruit, everybody left at the same time to go back to their respective cities. I'm not sure if that kind of get-together was normal for France or even for the culture of Madagascar, but it was far from the atmosphere that I'm used to in the US. I'm used to everyone showing up late, usually bringing no food or money for the guests, and everyone trying be the first to get crab legs or ribs before there's enough for everybody. This gathering was definitely beneficial for me to see that there's a different way to host and attend a cookout.

For my final days in Toulouse, I decided to stay in an Airbnb in Centre-ville, where it was much easier to get around the city and go to stores. The location was perfect, but the apartment building was old and far from being in the best condition. Besides being close to the downtown park, restaurants, and metro, I was right next to the area where the street market was held during the day.

The market was great because the fruit was usually fresh and inexpensive. It was also beneficial, being so close that I was able to listen to conversations and strengthen my French ordering skills. A bonus for patrons was that on certain days there was fresh fruit and vegetables that had to be left behind because the rules did not allow some vendors to sell them beyond a day or the weekend. Most people would be ashamed to say that they took some of these fruits and veggies for free, but if you could see how fresh this fruit still was, you would be in agreement with me.

My stay in downtown Toulouse was a great conclusion to my time in France, because the everyday hustle was over. I was able to savor the calm of the city one last time before I went back to the States. I went back to the Hoops Factory before I left, and it was great to speak with the staff as friends, thanking them for their help while I was in Toulouse. After some final French conversations, one of the guys said "T'es francais," which means that I was now accepted as French, and that he approved of my French vocabulary and grammar. I did not leave the country with a team for the next season like I had envisioned, but I made connections and friendships that would be sure to help me along my journey. I had only planned to stay in Toulouse for one month, but I wound up staying for six and was able to grow as a person, explore, and improve my French as well.

Conclusion

When I first made the decision to travel to my desired destinations instead of staying in the States, the initial motivation was the idea of getting away and seeing something different. However, the people and places that I encountered were far more than I could have even imagined. The ongoing fad in America is to turn yourself into a career worker and search for the unattainable illusion of being safe and secure. Many people have had financial success in their lives or are just in a position to take a trip, but they're still either too scared to take one, or they would rather feel safe by just holding onto their possessions. After my trip, I realized that the more we travel, the more we can learn about ourselves and other people. During this learning process, we can make the world smaller and also eradicate the stereotypes and incorrect perceptions that we have had about certain cultures.

Another fear that mentally blocks people from being able to travel is their perception of the level of safety in another country. I fully understand that Americans feel safer in America because they're more familiar with the cities and the majority of people speak English, but I'm sure that the US would not be on the top of the list of the safest countries. The truth is that no one is one hundred percent safe anywhere, and even though the US may be regarded as one of the richest countries, we still have huge safety problems that we live through every day. Major US cities have a huge problem with crime, specifically murder, but that does not stop most people from traveling there. Whenever you have questions about whether a country or specific city is safe, I recommend that you do a little research to see the problems, and find out if those problems are restricted to certain areas.

It has been stated that Paris was the world's most-traveled tourist destination before the terrorist attacks in November of 2015, but the terrorism resulted in a decrease of tourism. It's unfortunate that a tragic event resulted in the loss of lives and many injuries, and subsequently made France look unsafe. I happened to be in Paris in the October of 2015, and I left the day before the attacks with the impression that the City of Lights was the safest place in the world. I had literally walked in almost every neighborhood in the Paris, sometimes after midnight, and never had any problems. As such, when people ask me if Paris is safe, all I can give them is my stories of how good the people were to me and the fact that I've never had a problem. There are many websites that will provide safety level alerts and safety warnings for almost every country and city in the world, so I suggest that you peruse those outlets. The United States has a travel alert webpage, which is www.travel.state.gov/.

Solo travel requires a comfort level that you may have to grow into, so I do recommend traveling in a group the first time you leave the country. The first time I went to Europe, my sister, Joy, was living in London, and I went with my mother and my friend, Jadon, to visit her. The trip was smoother than it otherwise would have been because we knew someone who was living in the area, but also because we were a group of four. The second time I went out of the country, I planned a trip with my two friends, Alonzo and Marc, to Europe, and even though the planning process was difficult because of our lack of funds, the trip memories are endless. By going with a group, you have the opportunity to spread around the expenses and share the international experiences with multiple people.

A common misconception about travel is that everything has to be expensive, and that there are set margins for flights and hotels in certain areas. Any of my friends and family can tell you that I like to search high and low for the best price that can offer me a decent level of quality. I do not mind how fancy an airline is, as long as it gets me to my destination safely. I never stay in dirty hotels, but I'm also not looking for luxury when I travel. The airline industry has made some serious changes since I started traveling heavily in 2014, and, in my opinion, they benefit the customer. There are a variety of websites that have formulated great systems to help you find the most cost-efficient flight and/or hotel.

Once you get to a country, the different costs of goods or services will vary depending on where you go. Paris probably had the highest cost of living that I have experienced during my travels, but I understood that the quality of life was also higher. The cost of food may be slightly higher than the prices in America, but I'm sure that the majority of travelers would agree that the quality of even common food in France is higher than almost anywhere else. A key element that you have to consider when analyzing prices is to look at the different standards for goods and services in an area. Once I started living in several different cities for a month at a time, I began to understand that a lot of countries simply have higher standards for certain areas of their life. It's evident that other cultures value things differently than America—many times for the better.

Once I started traveling to different countries in Africa and explored areas that I hadn't really heard much about, I realized that you do not have to go to the well-known travel destinations to have a great time. Senegal and Zanzibar were two of my favorite destinations, and as a tourist, it was very inexpensive to enjoy my time there. For whatever reason, the countries in Africa have been a lost treasure, because Americans either just do not travel to them or only like to pick certain African countries that they feel are safe. A lot of the narrative about Africa in America is that all of Africa is dangerous and undeveloped, so it would make no sense to travel there. That couldn't be farther than the truth, and after my trips to different areas, I plan on traveling to more countries in Africa to get immersed in their cultures. There is a ton of information online that talks about all of the African countries. Therefore, it would be a great idea to look up countries that may be attractive to you.

For myself, I definitely was able to grow as a person and see life for much more than money and sports. My initial goal was to improve my French and find a basketball team so that I could get established in France. As I lived in France and other areas, I found that titles and labels do not really mean anything, and it's important to learn more about people each day. I had to go through some tough mental tests to understand lessons about how the world is much bigger than just the US, and that using my ingrained American thinking would not always work when I was abroad. The great people that I met along the way allowed me to see the kindness in human beings and realize that there are places around the world where everybody isn't only focused on themselves and money. I was amazed time and time again at how people naturally showed me genuine kindness that I rarely, if ever, experienced back home. I give much thanks to the countless, unnamed people who helped me with my French and Spanish in the supermarkets, butcheries, bakeries, and metro stops.

A new practice that I developed and plan to continue with was to force myself to speak to new people every day. It was not something I cared to do in America, and it was even more difficult to do while speaking French, but it was necessary because I had to get around the country. By improving my French and Spanish, I now listen better and actually pay attention to what people are saying. A lot of times we develop a habit of breezing through small talk conversations, but I had to lose that practice, instead focusing on trying to understand French and Spanish speakers. When I first arrived in Paris, many strangers would ask me a question and I would quickly say that I couldn't help them, simply because I could not understand what they were saying or did not have the confidence that I could direct them because of my limited French vocabulary. After a while, I challenged myself to stop, listen, and use the best French I could to help anybody who had a question for me.

The more I spoke to people and got to know them, I realized that I also had to decrease my default tough, nonchalant Philadelphian personality, because it did not really fit when I was in public in Europe and on the African continent. I had far too many strangers help me and smile excessively while I was still stuck in my laid-back, disinterested mindset. I know the stereotype Americans have about the French is that they are rude, but after forming friendships and speaking with strangers, I found that to be false. I came to Europe with a humble demeanor, and aside from a few street vendors, everyone I came in contact with never gave me an attitude for not being able to speak French. I'm pretty sure that it will be difficult to continue the humble, easygoing French attitude that I developed in Europe, but I'm sure it's possible.

The personal attitude change that I went through by speaking to Europeans was slightly different than the effect that Africans had on me. Between the Africans that I met in Europe and the Africans that I met in their respective countries, I was able to pick up the African pride that they all carried. No matter what social class I perceived them to be in, all the Africans I encountered and observed did not look like they were searching for some identity. The continuous search for an identity is something that I see Black Americans struggle with a lot in the US. It's quite obvious that most Africans know the origin of their ancestors, so they have more of a reason to identify with their culture and not look for validation from a name brand or title. Whenever I had a chance to speak to locals anywhere in the African countries, I could sense the calm and pride in their spirit, even if their financial situation may not have been the best.

The most vivid memories I have of African pride was the people that I spent a great amount of time with while I was in Europe. When I attended the final event at the Poitiers basketball tournament with Jimmy, he gave me insight on how some Africans speak with each other. Of course, it was a basketball tournament, but outside of the court, there was no sense of rivalry or animosity, just love. I'm one of the most competitive people you will ever meet, but I learned that the rivalry can end on the court, and basketball is just a game at the end of the day. Because of all of the things I learned, I knew that this African pride and serenity was something that I had to add to my personality and share with my family, friends, and people in America.

I have had the unique opportunity to grasp different cultures and build relationships in so many places in such a small time. I feel that it's my duty to share the stories with as many people as I can. I'm well aware that these experiences weren't only made for me and that there are many other people who want to travel, so I'm determined to do more to make sure they are able pursue those visions. This manuscript is only a group of stories and observations based on my personal travels, but there are many more places to travel, and I aim to make the world smaller by traveling to them.

THE AUTHOR

Mark A. Cooper II is a real estate investor, basketball player and coach, youth mentor, graduate of Hampton University, and new author. In his book, *The Power of The Passport: My Year Away From America,* Mark combines his love for basketball and travel while in Europe and on the continent of Africa. He shares his experiences, vivid stories, and unforgettable people during his year and a half away from America.

Mark left his job with the hopes of pursuing his dreams of seeing something different than his surroundings in Philadelphia, Twelve countries and sixteen international cities later, Mark encountered something far greater that what he could have imaged. Starting with an idea of playing basketball in Spain, the vision evolved into living in Paris, and also immersing himself in the culture of Senegal.

Mr. Cooper holds a Bachelor of Science degree in Marketing from Hampton University. He enjoys traveling, basketball, cooking, and mentoring and tutoring youth. He also enjoys playing the piano and writing music. His greatest desire is to see people leave their comfort zone and travel the world. When not living abroad, he lives in Philadelphia, Pennsylvania.